White Rose

Marian Silverman

Copyright © 2013 Marian Silverman

All rights reserved.

Print layout by eBooks by Barb for booknook.biz

DEDICATION

To: *Holly Go Lightly, Golden Retriever,*
Who would settle for no less than the best of me.

And to Burton,
My first playmate, mentor, and writing teacher.

Although we may have different perceptions of these events,
You will always be my *First Love*.

GRATITUDES

To: Sandra Shafton, my dear friend, whose support, love and vision prompted me to write these stories in the first place.

To: Lisa Mora, accomplished writer and editor, whose friendship, insights, and expertise encouraged me to reveal myself and my story. She improved the writer as well as the writing.

To: Laura Jacobs, friend and gifted writer, who convinced me that my stories could help others. Her natural editing skills and keen eye for detail helped to polish the final draft.

To: Ramona De Felice Long, Editor, who supported the notion of a collection of stories and offered encouragement, direction and the impetus I needed to finish it.

To: Kathie Cole, veteran nurse at UCLA's Medical Center who founded the People-Animal Connection Program in 1994. My eternal gratitude for recognizing the need for alternative health care and for opening hospital doors to the 'therapy' dog.

To: Pamela Dumond, author and friend, whose enthusiasm, experience and prodding was just what I needed.

And last, to my daughter, Terrie Silverman, writer, teacher and performance artist, who surrounded me with loving and steadfast support. She believed that I could write this book even when I was filled with self doubt.

Contents

Introduction...3
Prologue..5

PART I – MOTHER

Dead Canaries..9
Alley Cats...17
Bad Child...21
The Cellar..29
Saturdays with My Mother...33
Fanny..38
Last Conversation with my Mother......................................42
My Mother is Dying..48

PART II – THE MEN

Coney Island Memoirs..63
The Magical World of Suicide..66
A Room of my Own..71
Be Not Afeard...76
Welcome to Los Angeles...82
Good Luck, Paul, I Hope You Catch the Red Shadow.........92
If Your Father Doesn't Love You..100
White Rose..107
Thanks for Listening...129
Epilogue to a Funeral..135
Gratitude...137

PART III – HOLLY GO LIGHTLY

"Go Say Hello"..143
The Search for Perfection...147
Bad Dog..154

Dr. Holly...159
Keppel..168
My Worst Nightmare..172
Water Dog..179
Letting Go..184
Alone Again..191
Living with a Therapy Dog...199
Holly's Plane Ride...205
The End of the Journey..212

PART IV – THE FINAL GIFT

The Final Gift of Love..225
Reprise..233
Mother's Day...240

Epilogue...247

Author's Disclaimer: Words can sometimes injure those we care about and would choose not to hurt. Although we cannot recall words that have been spoken thoughtlessly, words that have been written down are forever shards of glass.

Apologies to anyone who might be offended by words not intended to inflict pain.

Introduction

WHEN I WAS SIXTEEN, I stood frozen in front of the leopard cage at the Central Park Zoo in New York City, watching the large cat pace back and forth on the cement floor. At first I thought of the fur coats that rich women wore, flashing large velvety black spots against an amber background. Then the animal turned and looked at me. I gazed into the depth of his golden eyes. I had seen leopards in zoos before. But this encounter was different. We stared at each other. I saw him look at me with an intelligence that could not be ignored. I realized, uncomfortably, that he knew I was looking at him. We were watching each other. And the thought that flashed into my mind was remarkable. There was someone in there.

A prisoner in a small concrete cage, he was left forever to pace without purpose or dignity simply because of the misfortune of his beauty and wildness. I saw in his haunted eyes the same look I had seen as a child of eight at the circus when I stared at the captive gorilla, and he stared back. I recognized the sorrow in those dark eyes.

This awareness foreshadowed the deep relationship I would have with animals throughout my life. As an adult, I rescued lost and abandoned dogs and cats on the streets of Los Angeles.

Unable to tolerate abuse in any form, I couldn't bear their suffering and their helplessness. I studied telepathic communication with an animal psychic in order to communicate with them, to find out who they were and what they thought and felt, and to learn how much like *me* they were. I swam with dolphins in Key Largo, Florida, in pools inevitably too small for these wild creatures, and shuddered that they too were exploited for our entertainment and, worst of all, that I had participated in their captivity.

Hybrid wolves confined to a few acres surrounded by invisible electric wires wakened me with their screams as they ran through the boundaries, willing to tolerate electric shock rather than give up their freedom and wildness. I visited Kenya to see firsthand the lions, giraffe, wildebeests, and other wildlife living in man-made reserves, and was shocked to realize that they too were attractions, changed by being watched, and that I willingly came as a tourist.

I studied animal behavior with the same compulsion that drove me to study human behavior, and to surround myself with vulnerable children as a teacher and School Psychologist. I wanted to understand how anyone could allow animal or children suffering. I wanted to know why I felt wounded.

I was intrigued by the interspecies connection, and realized that we need it to be fully human. I awakened to the idea that animals are authentic living beings, that they are honest in the moment, and that we have a deep and primal relationship with them. I saw a nobility in animals—a purity. This passion transformed and inspired my life.

It led me to find the companion dog that was destined to provide powerful healing energy to the disabled, diseased and depressed. Through her I would witness the human-animal bond at its highest level. Through her I would find purpose and healing in my own life.

Prologue

HER HAIR IS GOLDEN with a reddish cast, a strawberry blonde. Mine is faded blonde, with invasive gray at the temples that requires coloring. Well it doesn't require anything, but I choose not to be gray. I choose not to be old as well, but of course it is happening anyway. And it is happening to Holly. Except for her jet black nose, outlined mouth, and dark almond-shaped eyes shaded by golden lashes, her face is white up to and around the brows. Her crowning glory remains the honey gold floppy ears that match her coat and frame her beautiful face. I'm not sure who is aging faster. She is my companion, my working partner, the reason I get up in the morning, and the reason I return home at night. She is my Golden Retriever, Holly Go Lightly, named for the Audrey Hepburn character in *Breakfast at Tiffany's*.

She is the dog I wanted when I was seven years old and was denied anything four-footed in the house. She is the loss of all losses. She is more beloved than my mother when she died, than my father when he died, than David when he left me, each time he left me. She is my life line. She will die before me, unless I die very soon.

When the surgeons removed the spleen that had ruptured

from the weight of the cancer, they discovered two more cancers in her colon just in case the first one didn't kill her. Is that what they mean by over-kill? They cut her open on the last Thursday in February. They cut me open the same day. And I bled. And I bled. Malignancy: comes from the root *mal*, meaning 'bad'; malpractice, malnutrition, malformation, maligned, maladjusted, the bad kid in Harry Potter, Malfoy. Bad, bad, bad. When I leave any of my pets in the hospital, it is a bad omen. Sometimes I never see them again. I left without Holly. Very bad.

I have struggled to make everything right for her. I did my research on Goldens; nowhere did I find splenetic tumor. I read all the books, went to the best breeders, did all the training, and gained all I could know about this very first dog in my life. I wanted a healthy dog. She became sick. I wanted an obedient dog. She didn't listen to me. All my unresolved issues were played out with her. I was never assertive. I wanted to please her. I waited on her. I worshipped her. I thought you were supposed to give them choices. Do you want to go out and play now? What would you like? What do you need? Let me take care of you.

Holly taught me many things—most of all, how to take control of my life by learning how to take charge of her. I am still in process. It is not finished. But time up, game over. I love her and she is dying. And I cannot do a thing about it. We lie on the floor together on her comforter and I put her head in my lap, massage her shaven abdomen with the deep dark gashes that go from one end to the other, and I tell her how beautiful she is. She sleeps peacefully. I don't sleep at all. And never will again. I thought we would grow old together. But time has fast forwarded her into old age.

She is leaving me.

PART I

MOTHER

Dead Canaries

CHIPPY-JIMMY THE THIRD lay stiff at the bottom of his cage, his legs sticking straight up in the air like two twigs. I replaced the quilted night cover and gently smoothed it with my hands to keep the secret—another dead bird.

Canaries wake with the sun, and the males sing their songs until dark. Without light, they have a false sense of night and become quiet. I learned painfully that a covered cage in the middle of the afternoon meant the occupant was dead. My mother may have foolishly believed she was protecting me by keeping the evidence hidden, but of course it was one of many deceptions. When a person dies, we cover the body; it is now a corpse, and a clear signal that says death, not sleep. I knew at once that Chippy-Jimmy was another casualty in this house.

I walked into the kitchen and stood before my mother. I asked the same question I always asked. She was standing at the stove stirring something in a skillet.

"Please, Mommy, can I get a puppy? I'll take care of it, I promise."

"No dogs in this house," she said firmly. She had not wavered in her decision. She didn't mind birds as long as they were caged. My first pet was a yellow canary, a male, chosen by my father because the females didn't sing. In later years this would strike me as an irony in a home where females were considered of lesser value and were not allowed to be all they could be, like the songless female canaries. And I say canaries, plural, as each new offering didn't live very long. In one year, I discovered three dead birds lying feet up at the bottom of their cages. After the first two died, I realized that attachments were risky.

What I really wanted was a soft as down puppy to lick my face, hold in my arms and kiss on each floppy ear, a fluffy four-legged jolly creature with tail a wag who would trot after me happily down the street. I needed something warm and loving to hold in my arms and cuddle, someone that would look into my eyes with approval, someone who thought I was good and worthy, someone who wouldn't leave me. With a dog, I'd never be lonely again.

The canaries weren't dead when my father brought them home, but as if cursed, they all died imprisoned behind metal bars.

My mother grabbed my arm and dragged me across the street if she saw a dog approaching us. She said that I was bitten by a large black dog when I was two years old and put my hand in his mouth. I didn't remember that incident at all. I had no fear of dogs. My mother obviously did. And as long as I lived under her roof I was never allowed the puppy I longed for.

Since I was rarely allowed out of the house, the caged birds were brought in to be my companions. Girls were supposed to stay home with their mothers. My twelve-year-old brother sometimes kept me company, especially on rainy days. He resembled our Mom with his brown wavy hair and soft brown eyes. I always wondered who I looked like. I didn't think I belonged in this family, or had been switched in the hospital.

Many years later, my therapist summed it up. "You were

dropped down the wrong chimney." That explained a lot, and held no one to blame. It was a useful idea and made me feel better to hear that it wasn't my fault, or theirs. But since I had my father's green eyes, lean body, long fingers and blonde hair with reddish tones like his red moustache, these were probably my real parents.

My brother Robert didn't have the same experiences. It was as if we grew up in different homes with different parents. He was the lucky one. On sunny days he was sent outside to play softball in a dirt lot across the street, or hockey in the road on roller skates. I saw him flying by our front window wielding a broom handle for a hockey stick. I sat by that window facing the street so I could watch for him. I prayed for rain because then he would stay home and invent games to play with me.

Rob liked to make his own board games. He used cardboard boxes to design a football field with measured lines for downs earned, a baseball diamond with bases and home plate drawn in, and an ice hockey field with goals. He drew the spaces and lines and used tiny little figures to move around the board. We spun the pointer and moved our little markers that number of spaces on the board. Whoever reached the goal line or home plate first was the winner. I won as many games as he did since there was no skill involved and they were designed mostly to entertain me.

Sometimes in the middle of our game, he looked out the window, jumped up smiling, put the game away, and announced, "I'm going out now." It had stopped raining. And he was gone. I'd lost him again to the sunshine. My brother was the first one to break my heart. I was destined to be attracted to inaccessible men.

Some days I pushed my doll-carriage into the back yard. My little doll wore an organdy white dress like a bride, with a matching bonnet tied under her chin. Her wide blue eyes fluttered open when I held her up. The carriage looked like a real baby's coach, with large wheels and a collapsible hood to shade her face. Pushing it back and forth and rocking her to sleep made me feel like a mother. I kept her covered with a pink blanket, tucked her in, closed her eyes, and kissed her. "You're a good baby," I said.

My mother watched me from the upstairs back window while hanging the wet laundry on the clothes line, which extended from the window sill all the way across the yard to the telephone pole about fifty feet away. I was not allowed to leave the back yard.

I took care of my canary too. I fed him bird seed and lettuce, filled his water dish every day, and gave him white bread soaked in milk. Once a week, I cleaned the cage, washing the yellow droppings off his wooden perches and bars while he stayed in a little box. He didn't like the box and fluttered in frustration.

"Chippy-Jimmy, just wait," I told him. "I promise to let you out as soon as I can." I hated doing this to him, but I was told I had to clean his cage. It was my job.

On Saturdays, I was allowed to sit on the steps of the front stoop with my friend Maxine, who was also seven. She was the prettiest girl I knew, with long brown curls that bounced every time she turned her head from side to side. Cradled in her arms was a small white puppy with brown patches on his back and a tawny splash of color on each of his floppy ears. She squeezed him tightly until he squeaked like a toy.

"Do you want to pet him?" she asked. I touched his neck lightly with my fingers. He looked at me, his large brown eyes meeting mine. His tail wagged back and forth in rhythm like the metronome that sat on top of my piano when I practiced my scales. I slid my hand down his back all the way to his wiggly tail. He felt warm and his skin rippled under my touch. Then he licked my face, and it tickled.

"Do you like him?" she asked.

"Better than anything in the world," I answered.

On a blustery day in January, I walked home from school alone because my brother had gone ahead with his friends. My shiny black galoshes sank into the crunchy snow leaving deep reminders that I had been there. Keeping my head down as protection from the wind, I heard a whimper. Kneeling, I moved aside some fallen branches and twigs with my mittens. There in a mound of snow lay a quivering, cold body, its mouth gaping like a baby howling for its mother.

"A puppy!" I called out excitedly to no one. I scooped him up and brushed the snow off his fur, slipping him inside my winter coat next to my warmth. The whimpering stopped.

"You're safe," I told him. Now to smuggle him home and hide him from my mother. I went directly to the basement, and entered the dark *scary* cellar. My brother, already home, joined me and became a willing accomplice. "Don't tell Mom," he cautioned me. But I didn't need his warning. We had done this before with dismal results. Undaunted by our past failures, we filled a cardboard box with rags and old blankets to create a cozy bed, hid the little orphan in the warmest part of the cellar near the coal furnace, and prayed he wouldn't cry during the night. We gave him some warm milk, not knowing what else he needed. He was black as the coal in the bin and hard to see in the dark, except for a white diamond in the center of his forehead and four white paws illuminated by the dying coal embers. I kissed him right on that diamond and whispered, "Be good and be quiet." Then we went upstairs to pretend that nothing special had happened.

During the night, I heard those same cries of a baby, whimpering and whining. My mother heard them too. This was not the first puppy that had cried in the cellar.

In her long pink flannel nightgown, she poked her head into my bedroom. "Did you bring home another dog?" she said in an impatient voice.

"It's not a dog, it's a cold puppy," I said.

"Well, it has to go in the morning." She was already turning away, pulling the door closed behind her.

"Please, Mommy, can I keep it? I called out.

"No dogs" echoed in the hallway separating our bedrooms.

After this scene I was compensated with another terminal bird destined for back yard burial in a small jewelry box. The birds lived six months or less, dying from the cold drafts in our under-heated house in Brooklyn. My father shoveled coal every morning to stoke the furnace. In his efforts to conserve as much coal as possible, the house was cold overnight. The fragile canaries didn't have a chance.

My brother and I were sent to bed early to keep warm, slipping under the covers and listening to our radios in separate bedrooms until it was time for sleep. For me, this meant after *The Lone Ranger* was over, about eight o'clock every night. When I heard the theme music, which I know now is the "William Tell Overture," and the final "Hi ho, Silver," I turned off the lamp next to my bed. Since he was older, Rob listened to his radio for another hour. Through the thin wall separating our rooms, I lay awake listening too.

On Wednesday nights, I heard *The George Burns and Gracie Allen Show*, and laughed out loud at Gracie's absurd answers to her husband's questions. I thought Rob must have heard me laughing as he turned up the volume of his radio. "Say goodnight, Gracie" was the signature line that ended the program. My father once told me he had seen their vaudeville acts use that same hook to get them off the stage. In years to come they would close their television show with this line, until Gracie's death ended the act, a final good night.

When I was older and heard my mother say funny or silly

things, like when we played gin rummy and she called out "gin," but then refused to show her hand, laughing, "Do I have to prove it?" I teased, "Say goodnight, Gracie." She smiled at me, her beautiful smile. My mother was many things.

At nine o'clock, it was lights out for everyone in the house. The canary cage was covered. My dad looked into each bedroom to be sure we were going to sleep and not reading under the covers. He also made his nightly rounds into each bedroom to pour water into a metal container hanging over the radiator to keep the air moist as we slept. Then he went down to the cellar to bank the fire in the furnace. He must have known we hid puppies in the cellar, but said nothing. Unlike my mother, he liked dogs, and grew up with a dog named Spot. I never thought my father liked me very much, at least he never showed me any affection, but I suspect he would have let me have a puppy if not for my mom.

On school days, I arrived home at 3:15, already listening for the chirping of my little bird as I climbed the stairs. My parents owned the building, rented out the downstairs, and we lived in the apartment above because it had more light and heat. My mother hovered near the kitchen table reminding me to have my glass of milk and three freshly baked and still warm cookies. My brother was not home yet. He liked to hang out after school with his twelve-year-old friends. They were in a club called The Bullets A.C., which stood for athletic club. They all wore matching blue jackets with the club logo of bullets on the back. He was the president of the club because he was the only one with a basement and a ping pong table.

In the living room, I sat down on the hard wooden bench in front of the piano that had Baldwin on the front and was slightly out of tune, to practice my two-handed scales and simple songs. I turned on the metronome that clicked back and forth keeping the metered time. The bird cage hung on a stand right above the piano in front of the living room window. Chippy-Jimmy sat on his perch, warmed by the afternoon sun's rays that peeked through the Venetian blinds. I looked up at him cleaning and preening his feathers with his little beak while balancing by wrapping his twig like toes around the narrow wooden perch. His head cocked to one side, one eye looking at me, as if he was waiting for his cue to join in. I began to play my little song. His chest puffed up as he sang in accompaniment. And so we had our daily concert. He warbled sweet high octave notes, his whole body trembling with the vibrations of the song.

One day I heard no singing on the stairs. I entered the living room to see the bird cage still covered in the middle of the day. There was not a sound in the room.

"Why is the bird cage covered?" I asked my mother, hoping for the truth this time. "Oh, he's still sleeping," she lied. It was a familiar scene, one to which I had grown accustomed. I shed no tears.

Everything caged dies.

WHAT PSYCHOLOGISTS CALL "PRE-COGNITIVE *commitment" tells what happens to flies raised in a jar when the lid is finally removed. They continue to buzz around the jar with no attempt to escape out of the opening. They no longer recognize freedom. It is not in their perception to have this choice. Cats, born and raised in cages with vertical bars become blind to horizontals. When released they bump into anything horizontal. So it was with my perception of the world. When I grew up and physically left home, I continued to buzz around my caged world with no idea that I could fly away and change everything.*

Alley Cats

After the death of Chippy-Jimmy the 3rd, my father stopped bringing home canaries. "Those birds are too sickly," he said.

I wanted to yell, "No! There is nothing wrong with them. They are dying from catching cold in an unheated house so that you can save money on coal." But I knew better than to contradict my father. He had to be right about everything.

Thank god, I thought. No more coming home dreading the sight of another covered cage; no more having to see my sweet yellow birds lying stiffly at the bottom of their cages, no more dead canaries.

Although I missed the singing, the sweet chirping soprano tones that made their puffed up chests vibrate whenever I played the piano, what I really wanted wasn't a caged bird. I longed for the puppy who would never leave me, and who would love me forever.

It was bad enough that my mother banned animals from the house. One evening I saw her attempt to murder the homeless cats that lived in the alleys and cellars in the neighborhood. I watched her roll up the kitchen window, lean out and carefully pour a steaming kettle of water two stories down to scatter the alley cats.

The yowls of alarm sent me running to the open window. I looked down to the driveway and felt my stomach drop. They were gone.

"What happened to the cats?" I asked her, horrified.

"We had to get rid of them," she said matter-of-factly. "They make too much noise at night."

True to her word, I never again heard the nightly wails. I couldn't believe that she would "get rid of them." She considered cats particularly nasty, like vermin, and as abhorrent as the rodents my father caught in those springed death traps. Together they would rid the house of all pests. Like the squirming mice pinned to wooden planks and suffering a slow death in the early hours before my father got up and drowned them in the toilet, I discovered that I wasn't wanted here either. *She would get rid of me too.*

The morning sunlight peeked through the kitchen blinds, lighting up the pink walls. My pretty mother in her starched housedress and wearing no make-up, her bobbed brown hair falling over one eye like the movie stars of the 40's, did what other Jewish mothers in Brooklyn did to discipline their children. They threatened them.

My Aunt Estelle bragged that she made my three young cousins behave by saying "If you don't stop it right now, I'm calling Dr. Brown." Doctors made house-visits and appeared as frightening intruders coming into the child's bedroom to sit on the edge of the bed. This scary man unbuttoned pajama tops, and poked and prodded and thumped with his cold hands. He always prescribed horrid tasting medicines and ordered the child to stay in bed and not be allowed outside until he could come back and check him again. It was a prison sentence.

All children in our family were afraid of Dr. Brown and those words, "I'm calling Dr. Brown," were lethal weapons for discipline. When my cousins were really sick and the dreaded doctor appeared, their parents were embarrassed by a child screaming at the very sight of the "bogey-man."

My mother, more creative than that, devised her own fail proof system. What is the most terrifying threat to a young child? Worse than a doctor, or a spanking, or being yelled at? She knew. It was the fear of abandonment. It was primal. And she used it.

She spoke into the phone in a calm voice, while I glared at her, my heart pounding in my chest. "Hello? Is this the New York Department of Correction?—I have a bad child." She fixed her deep-set brown eyes on me as I huddled in the corner by the kitchen stove, terrified.

"Can you come and pick her up today?" she said.

I feared for my life.

She perched on the barstool in front of the window, her thighs crossed casually as she pressed the receiver against her ear, listening for an answer. I didn't notice that she held down the disconnect button. I figured that out years later since no one ever came to take me away. But at the time, I believed every word. She would get rid of me just like the annoying alley cats. I was bad. She didn't want me either.

With matted blonde hair pasted to my face, wet with tears, I crept across the spotless kitchen floor on my hands and knees toward my mother and threw myself at her feet.

"I'll be good. Don't send me away," I whispered, choking on the words, trying not to cry out loud, or scream, or beg. She didn't move, just stared at me. Lying on the cold linoleum, I screamed, "Please Mommy, I'll be good." The chicken soup simmered on the stove top, while smells of home and mother mingled with the perspiration of my fear.

I had no idea what being good was, or how to do it, but my screaming seemed to placate her. She hung up the phone...until the next time. It was all a scare tactic and it worked perfectly. I was frightened out of my wits by her uncanny power to dispose of annoyances, like the puppies that were given to anyone who wanted them and the alley cats that were doused with scalding water and the mice who died a terrible death pinned to traps.

For the rest of my life I would search for ways to be good. I would always feel sorry for unwanted animals.

Bad Child

GROWING UP IN AN insane family was not all bad. Sometimes I think it's the advantage I have over others who thought or imagined they had normalcy. It's certainly where my sense of humor comes from. Laughter was my survival. Laugh or go under were the two choices. Although there were parts that I never understood, and so much that still haunts me, there is something comical about it all.

My mother was a case in point. She played at being naive, but was crafty. There was always a method to her madness. She actually believed that raising children was like growing plants. If you watered them and fed them and spoke to them occasionally, they would grow. So we were fed, my brother and I, at least until I stopped eating her food.

And although I really only wanted to be acceptable, normal, maybe even valued, what I didn't get was that this was not in the script. The script called for a defective child, a role assigned to me, and a good and responsible and valued child, my brother, and parents who were to orchestrate the interaction and remediation of the defective child in order that they could feel powerful, in control and effective; most of all effective. For unless you have a cause, and someone to rescue, you may not attain these attributes.

So I played my part to the hilt. I was sick a lot, I was dumb a lot, and I was needy a lot. What an opportunity for them to help me. Wow! They were so good at it. Everyone in the family saw what good, caring and nurturing folk they were. This child was such a problem! It would take time and talent to help her. So when I stopped eating, it really got their attention.

Now at last they had a terrific cause. No one knew about anorexia, so I was diagnosed as "bad." Much simpler. The less I ate, the more they focused on my problem behavior. And I felt that it was better to be wanted by the police than not to be wanted at all. But the truth is, I simply was not hungry. Although the glorious (I am told) smells of my mother's cooking filled the house, for me it was nauseating, and unappetizing. I became the family focus. I got more attention from not eating than anything else I did. I didn't eat for years.

All I really wanted was for them to like me. Forget love me, I'd have settled for like. My brother, on the other hand, seemed to exude okayness. He was certainly the good child, the one they liked. In fact he was part of the plot to keep me feeling inadequate. I only realized many years later that Robert's survival depended on my weakness. He had taken on the attributes of the prison guards, as in the Stockholm Syndrome. And I now understand that he paid a high price for the title of good child. It was easier to be bad.

Yet I was devastated when he left home (and me) to get married. How could he leave me with them? Somehow I thought it was us against them, and that I was part of the "us." Wrong!

I was always alone.

In every family, children are assigned roles early and carry them for life. In my home, my brother was clearly the good child. He did what he was told. He never argued with his parents. Rob went on to become the good son, good husband, good father. If he were a canine he would be a gentle collie, always loyal and devoted to his family. My role was defined differently.

I was not a good child. Good children eat their mother's food. Good children do what they are told. There was a time when I ate, but never enough to satisfy her. She was always pushing more at me. It was nothing less than pure irony that I refused to eat the food of a mother known all over Brooklyn for her authentic Jewish cooking.

"No, thank you, I don't want any more," didn't stop the onslaught of extra helpings of mashed potatoes that were shoveled onto my plate.

"Oh yes," she said sweetly, "you know you want some more," while dumping even more food into my plate. Our house smelled of sweet and sour stuffed cabbage, pot roast with roasted potatoes, raisin and apple-filled luxun puddings, and her pastry rolls filled with fruits, walnuts and brown sugar.

"I'm not hungry, I'm not hungry," screamed in my head. It was futile to say these words out loud. No one ever heard me. I still tend to repeat myself, making the same point over and over as if no one was listening. Some friends say I nag. I tend to think no one really hears me.

I sat alone at the table, food still on my plate. My mother instructed me in a firm voice, "Sit there until you eat." With glazed eyes, I stared numbly at the food, holding my head up with both elbows on the rose-bud oil cloth that covered the kitchen table. When my arms got tired, I fell asleep with my head nearly flopping into the brisket. Eventually, it was bedtime and I was allowed to leave the kitchen.

Mornings were even worse. "You can't go to school until you eat your oatmeal," she said. "You need something to stick to your ribs." She placed the bowl of thick, lumpy, mush in front of me. I tried to eat it. I dipped in my spoon and put a little of it in my mouth. Revulsed, I gagged on the lumps and spit it out into the bowl. With no hesitation, she whisked the bowl away and from the pot of cooked oatmeal on the stove, she filled another bowl. The result was the same. I couldn't get it down. Finally, she let me go. The nausea and putrid taste stayed in my mouth all the way to school.

There is a special odor to a brand new coloring book; maybe it's the printer's ink, or the paper. But that smell is recorded in my memory as the bribe for eating food I didn't want in my mother's kitchen. If I finished the food on the plate in front of me, my father would take me to "the 5 & 10" and let me choose a big fat coloring book. I liked the ones about little girls who were punished, or misunderstood: Snow White, Sleeping Beauty or Cinderella.

I was a really good colorer, but not a good eater. It took me a long time, but eventually a collection of coloring books began to appear in a stack on the floor of my closet in my tiny bedroom. My father seemed to take pride in bragging to anyone visiting, and would even bring them into my bedroom, pointing to the pile on the floor as if they were nothing less than works of art. I didn't feel flattered at all.

What's so great about coloring inside the lines?

Eat your food and do what you're told to do. Just like my life. So I outlined the figures with a bold black crayon to make sure my crayon did not waver or be tempted to create anything that wasn't prescribed; these were the rules of coloring. Stay in the lines. My boundaries were clearly drawn for me and there was to be no transgressing. Don't break the house rules. I had to work hard for those rewards. I had to work to get the food down before bedtime.

The school personnel went crazy. Each semester they weighed and measured us in the girls' gymnasium. The P.E. teacher would announce that I had grown another inch, but was not gaining weight. By age twelve, I was five feet four, and weighed seventy-two pounds. This was reported to child services and they sent a social worker to our house. She arrived without an appointment and stood there ringing the doorbell until my mother, wearing her perennial house-dress with the yellow tea-roses on it, opened the door.

"Can I help you?" she said. My mother expected this woman to be collecting money for the church or some cause and didn't at first invite her to come in.

The woman introduced herself while I stood silent in the corner of the room feeling nauseated. I was in trouble again. The social worker was very prim. She wore a black suit and flat heeled shoes and carried a stack of papers and folders.

"We're concerned about why your daughter is so thin," she began, frowning. "Does your family need financial help of some kind?" She looked worried.

My mother's face turned red with anger and embarrassment. "Please come in," she said sternly and marched into the kitchen. She wildly threw open the kitchen cabinets to reveal shelves of canned and packaged food. She opened the ice box to show the variety of cheeses, and assortment of fresh vegetables, and her home-made casseroles, even a calf's tongue sticking out, an icebox crammed with dinners that would have fed more than a family of just four.

"She won't eat," was all she could say to defend herself from this accusation.

When the woman left, satisfied that we didn't need relief money, my mother turned to me coldly. "They think I don't feed you. They don't know you're just bad."

Good children eat their mother's food.

I looked down, hung my head and had no answer. The sick

feeling when she forced me to eat oatmeal returned. I would not eat her food at dinner that night.

The doctor prescribed a horrible tasting red "tonic" to give me an appetite. My mother would hold out the liquid on a tablespoon twice a day before meals.

"Take it already, my arm is getting tired," she would say in exasperation. I swallowed it, making a face of disgust, and then I spit it out. Predictably, I was given another spoonful. I still cannot drink red wine because the color and the bitter taste remind me of those tonics.

I was anorexic before anyone knew what that meant. The doctors told my mother to feed me anything I wanted, anytime I wanted it. I wasn't hungry in that house. Yet on Sundays, my Jewish mother, who still kept a kosher kitchen, cooked something I did like, bacon strips.

They were just for me. For this she pulled out a heavy black skillet used exclusively for the forbidden food, and a metal plate and fork, the kind used for camping, She burned the bacon to be sure it was well cooked, so there was always bacon smoke in the kitchen. I sat at the table and ate all of the curly charred strips on my plate.

Sometimes on Sunday morning, she would look out of the window and see my grandmother coming down the street, unannounced. My Jewish grandmother for whom there would be no explanation that would suffice. My mother sprang into action, opening all the windows, and waving her hands and newspapers around wildly trying to get the smells out in time. The utensils were thrown into the old washboard section of the sink that had a cover on it and could be hidden. I'm surprised she didn't wash my mouth out, so thorough was her clean-up. And when at last my grandmother entered the house, climbed the stairs and arrived in the kitchen, there wasn't a trace of bacon or dishes, but bacon smell, that's something else. She would say something in Yiddish to my mother, and I never knew if she really didn't know, or was pretending she didn't smell it, because she loved me and wanted me to have it. I still love bacon.

Threatening to "give me away" was the only discipline I remember. My parents never hit me. Robert, five years older was told, "Take care of your sister." If I came home from school crying, he would go after the kid who dared to throw a snowball at me. He would go after them physically. He was my protector, my hero. He also was my abuser.

When they came home, they found me with bruises on my arm. I was five years old. He was ten. I told them, "Robert hit me." My mother fretted, "To think that my children should hate each other."

Nothing was done.

My brother hit me when he was frustrated. He hit me when I said things to him that he didn't like. If I presented a not-so-good-report card, B's and C's instead of A's, he took me into my bedroom and closed the door to discuss the poor grades and straighten me out. With a sad, 'it's for your own good' face, he punched me hard in the arm, or smacked the side of my head. "Don't you know you're upsetting Mom with that C? You have to do better."

He was the big brother in charge of keeping me in line. My parents never hit me. But he was allowed, maybe encouraged to do it, since they would not. A Sergeant at Arms, he reported directly back to them after he had followed the orders of the house.

I never heard that this was wrong. No one ever said I didn't deserve to be beaten up. I needed to hear that. What I heard was that this is what brothers did to little sisters. So this was normal. He continued to be physical with me. I was verbal with him. I learned how to make words cut, my only weapon. I thought I deserved to be hit for what I would say. It was my fault. And nothing was done.

Where were my loving parents? Why was this okay? Why did I have to handle it alone? Where were my advocates? Didn't I deserve advocates?

I learned to remain in difficult situations. No one was going to help me, so I never asked for help. You stay, no matter what—you try to make it work, no matter what. Why didn't anyone teach me to save myself first? I learned that you don't have the right to say this hurts, or it isn't good for me. You take whatever comes. You deserve whatever happens. Somehow you brought it upon yourself.

I was destined to be a battered wife at the worst of it, barely escaping with my life, and at best a suffering woman in love with a man who would repeatedly betray my love and trust by leaving me.

My brother was the one who cared about me, which prepared me for being battered in a marriage, where I was straightened out and cared about in much the same way and for the same reason. I was bad and deserved it.

And nothing was done to save me. Nothing was done.

The Cellar

THE LOCKED DOOR THAT led to the cellar in our house reminded me of the attic that imprisoned the deranged wife in *Jane Eyre*. I never went in alone; in fact, I avoided going in there at all. It was the basement, grounded underneath our two-story, two-family brick home. I awoke every morning to a chilled house, where I huddled under the covers and listened to the sound of my father shoveling coal. The cellar was used to store a mountainous pile of blue-black coal stacked beneath a high window where it was delivered down a chute into the bin. This was our heating system.

Daddy would start a fire in the huge blackened stove-like oven with newspaper, then when the coal ignited, the heat from the fire traveled through the pipes and into the radiators in the house. I could hear the clanging of the metal radiators as they started to heat up in each room.

The cellar housed additional rooms the length of our house which mostly, as far as I could tell, stored junk" old tables, chairs, lamps, and assorted storage cartons. The only thing I enjoyed was an old trunk filled with costumes, and relics of my mother's childhood—things to dress up in, like a fox stole with the actual head of the fox (now I find this abhorrent); long evening dresses with sequined trimming; funny flapper hats; and gold beaded evening purses that were dazzling with long fringes.

I would get someone to go with me during daytime hours to retrieve any of these for play and dress up shows. There was very little lighting in the cellar. Each room had a single bulb swinging from the ceiling on a long cord. Maybe it was the darkness or the scary genre of "down in the cellar" movies that conjured up demons and monsters lurking down there. Frankenstein and the Wolf-Man at the Saturday film matinees my brother and I were sent to frightened me so much, I hid my face under my coat.

Sometimes at night, I thought I heard noises below; probably just mice running, but that was not a comfort either. I would imagine Frankenstein coming upstairs to "get" me. Given my feelings about the place, it isn't all that surprising that it was the unhappy site of a recurrent nightmare. I have read that recurrent dreams suggest some unfinished issue in your life. The dream recurred for many years, and was unchanging.

It always began the same: my father left the house in the morning to go to work, and immediately my mother became "the witch.' She wasn't exactly the Wicked Witch of the North from Oz —no long pointy nose or green face—but she looked evil nonetheless. She had my mother's face, but the angles were sharper, the hair was wilder, and she was ugly and shrieking at me. I knew at once she was a witch.

She dragged me, kicking and screaming, downstairs to the dreaded cellar, tied me to a chair with a Venetian blind cord, and left me there in the dark while I pleaded and screamed for my real mother to come.

"Stay there," said the witch. "You're a bad child."

The "good" mother never did come, and I stayed there, terrified and struggling against the cord that dug into my arms and legs. I was a captive in the chair all day until at night, my father found me, untied me, and returned me to the house upstairs, and to my real mother. I don't remember ever telling him what she had done. I accepted the rescue.

It felt like I really had two mothers, the witch and the good one. But the witch only appeared when my father was gone, so he never knew. The star of the dream was certainly my mother, who appeared in a dual role. My father, strangely enough, appeared as my rescuer, a role different than the oppressor I felt him to be in real life. When I awakened in my bed, I felt dazed and imagined it had been real and not a dream. It was disconcerting enough to make me wonder who these people really were.

My mother's weekly ritual of phoning the New York Department of Correction to ask them to come and take me away was not a dream. I never knew why I was bad but I believed her.

My father had a propensity to point out my inadequacies. "Oh, that's too hard for you. Here, let me do it, " he said, pulling the jigsaw puzzle pieces from my hands. It was a simple puzzle. I watched quietly as he put all the pieces in. I didn't have a chance. I must have been too stupid to do anything right. But worst of all, I thought my father really didn't like me. In my dreams I created a fantasy daddy, the hero I needed. He would save me.

The same nightmare continued for many years. The horror of this wasn't that my mother turned into a witch. I think I already knew that she wore two faces. The horror was that she abandoned me in the place I dreaded the most—this dark, demonical dungeon, where the monsters live.

ALTHOUGH I DON'T HAVE this dream anymore, there are other demons in my life, and often they appear to be friendly. But I am never really sure if lurking underneath their benign demeanor is something perhaps dangerous. I don't get close enough to find out. They are simply not to be trusted. I vowed that I would never allow anyone to tie me up and leave me alone in a dark cellar. But I did—at least metaphorically.

Saturdays with My Mother

My grandfather, a Jewish immigrant from Austria, believed as did many of his generation, that girls should not have careers—they should stay at home and become housewives and mothers. My mother had begged to go to nursing school, but my grandfather wouldn't hear of it. He said being a wife and mother was enough for any woman. Still, my mother longed to nurse someone, and I unwittingly gave her that opportunity.

The family knew of my mother's calling and Uncle Jack, the jokester, nick-named her Nurse Evans. When any of her nieces and nephews became ill, they would call for Nurse Evans, and she would arrive, even before the doctor. It was clear I needed to be sick for my mother to be happy.

When I was thirteen, she got her wish. Dr. Edelstein, the family physician diagnosed my chest cold as bronchitis and I was put to bed—indefinitely. Weeks of wheezing and coughing stretched into two months of being confined to my bed. Lying down made breathing more difficult, even with several propped up pillows, so my mother would sit on my bed all night leaning her back against mine. I gasped for air.

She would have breathed for me if she could.

Family and neighbors came to look at me, and bring me food

I didn't want. My brother came into the sick room with tears behind his eyelids. I thought that I must be dying. During the day, they moved me into his sunny bedroom and propped me up near a window to get the sun and air like a tuberculosis patient. My mother went to my school once a week to get the homework. I lost interest in school and had no friends visiting. I had only my mother, the full time nurse. I was dependent on her for my life.

Summer brought the end of the school year. Then something remarkable happened. On a warm Saturday morning, she got me out of bed and helped me into a dress, cotton stockings, and my holiday patent leather shoes. We went on the subway to see "The Park Avenue Specialist, Dr. Kugelmas." For a child who is usually under tight surveillance, never sent to summer camp, and required to come straight home after school, this was an adventure.

We boarded the train at Sheepshead Bay station, rode the BMT all the way into Manhattan, about an hour, then changed trains at 42nd street to the Lexington Avenue Line and got off at Park Avenue. This upscale street, with doormen at each building, women in furs walking or carrying their little fluffy pedigreed dogs, were a long way from Sheepshead Bay in Brooklyn.

It turned out that Dr. Kugelmas was an allergist; a new kind of specialist. This was the 1940's. How did my mother know about allergies? How did she find him? And how did she find the money to pay him on my father's fixed government salary? These are the questions I still wonder about. But I was grateful she let me get out of bed.

We were brought into a dark leathery waiting room, and then to a wood paneled office with the largest desk I'd ever seen. The doctor was seated behind it in a tall reclining swivel chair. He looked like the president of a bank. He was dark, forty-ish (about my mother's age), with thick black eyebrows and hair on his hands. After making numerous scratches all over my back, and listening to my raspy breath, he announced that I was allergic to everything that grew, walked or blew in.

He said, "This is not bronchitis. She has asthma. Get her out of bed." My heart leaped for joy. He gave me a special non-allergenic diet: no sauces, no spices, no fish, no tomatoes, no chocolate. I was told to eat rye krisp instead of wheat, and goat's milk instead of dairy. Ugh! The only foods I loved were tomatoes, and tomato sauce and ketchup, all forbidden now. I also craved herring in sour cream. That was definitely out.

I liked this man who told my mother to release me from my confinement. He also instructed her to rid my room of dust and feathers. Down came the long dusty drapes that kept out the light, while bedding and pillows were covered with plastic, and the carpeting was ripped up, leaving a nice hardwood floor. My room was clean and bright.

But the best part, and what I remember vividly, was coming into the city on the subway on Saturdays with my mother, the two of us in dresses and stockings held up by garters in the days before panty hose had been invented. We would make an entire day out of this doctor visit. My mother began to wear just a trace of rouge on her cheeks, and lipstick to match. This was a woman who wore no makeup and usually made no effort with clothes or fashion. She was a housewife, without a career or education. Her life was cooking and cleaning, playing maj jong afternoons, making do on my father's salary as a postal employee, and taking care of her two children, mostly me, the problem child, the one that didn't eat, and now wasn't breathing right.

Dr. Kugelmas flirted with my mother at each visit. He looked at me, a very thin, flat-chested thirteen-year-old with "dirty-blonde" hair to my shoulders and a bump on my nose from being hit in the face by my brother's baseball. I would make sure that bump was straightened in another three years, and I would pay for it out of my baby-sitting money. My parents would never approve cosmetic surgery, or "changing nature" as my father put it.

Dr. K. said, "You're a pretty girl, but you'll never be as good-looking as your mother." I saw her blush past the glow of the rouge on her cheeks.

On the way home, I asked her if she was planning to run away with him. I said, "Mom, he's rich, and he likes you. Maybe he'll ask you to leave Daddy and marry him." All she did was smile. She said nothing.

The possibilities of change and a better life appealed to me. Maybe if it happened to her, it could happen to me. After all, here we were on Park Avenue seeing an expensive specialist who thought my mother was pretty. She was flattered, and maybe more than that.

After the doctor visit, we went to "Chock Full O'Nuts," a building as sparkling white on the outside as its immaculately clean interior, a fast food restaurant that was part of a famous chain in New York. We sat on bar stools at the counter, and ate cream cheese sandwiches with dark nut and raisin bread, and yes, she let me eat the cream cheese even though it was dairy. This was one of those times I remember enjoying food. My mother didn't cook it, serve it, or shove it at me. Eating here was not an ordeal. We drank freshly squeezed orange juice, and had to get right up when we finished eating because there were people standing behind us waiting for our seats. Everyone was polite and friendly in Chock Full O'Nuts.

After that we'd go window shopping. I loved to look at the bridal gowns in those beautiful choreographed windows on Madison Avenue. We'd cut down a side street which was crowded with bridal shops one after another. She knew I loved to look at brides. She pretended it was just for me, but I suspect that she enjoyed looking and fantasizing also. We "oohed" and "aahed" over the satin and lace gowns with long trails modeled by dark haired, red-lipped mannequins. We stood in front of the store windows for a long time, each with our own thoughts, just gazing at the shimmering hopeful brides-to-be as they stood frozen in poses for weddings that would never be.

I dreamed of a wedding where I'd wear one of these gowns. Maybe she had her dream too. Did she fantasize having a different life than the one with my father? Did she dream of a life full of romance, adventure, luxury—a life with Dr. Kugelmas?

My mother and I continued to spend Saturdays in this way: Dr. Kugelmas, Chock Full O'Nuts, and window shopping. Sometimes we'd go into a large department store and look at clothes or housewares or furniture. We never bought a thing, just looked. It was never about buying or having. It was just about looking and dreaming. Anything seemed possible.

Fanny

I REMEMBERED THE SMELL of her, sweet like the honeysuckle blossoms that grew all around our house, the feel of her skin, soft as silk, and the color of chocolate. For years I had a recurring dream or memory where I felt warm loving arms lift me out of the bathtub and wrap me in towels, caressing every inch of me as this person, this "she" warmed and dried my little body. She gave me kisses, from my head to the bottoms of my feet. She was not my mother.

"Suzie, who is that?"

"Nanny," smiled the baby in my arms, while her parents, and my parents, laughed and clapped their hands. My little niece opened that sweet mouth of newly formed tiny white baby teeth and identified her grandmother, my mother, for the first time by name. I had spent that day teaching her to say "Nanny."

When I had a child, I made sure my daughter also learned to call my mother Nanny. And she was a nanny, adored by all of her grandchildren, as loving, nurturing, supportive and uncritical as any true nanny should be. But she was not my nanny.

One chilly morning in early winter, as we stood on the subway platform waiting for our train back to Brooklyn, all bundled into our woolen coats and scarves and gloves, I was startled to hear my mother yell out, "Fanny, Fanny!"

Across the tracks, on the opposite train platform stood a tall woman wearing an emerald-colored felt hat with a bird's feather sticking out of it, and a long black winter coat that came down to her ankles. She looked right at us, smiled the biggest broadest smile I had ever seen, white teeth gleaming in a chocolate brown face, and waved both of her arms in the air from side to side. Seconds later the train pulled into the station obscuring our view. And she was gone.

"Who was that?" I asked.

My mother didn't answer immediately. She looked at the train standing stubbornly in the station, totally blocking and denying us any further view or contact with this woman. She had probably boarded and disappeared into the abyss of frantic bodies scrambling for seats. My mother nervously pulled off one of her gloves, and then the other one, and held them in her hand as if she wanted to wave or throw them, but it was too late to do anything. She sighed and put them in her purse as the train began to move away from the station. I watched the train windows for another glimpse of this woman, but the dirty windows moved faster and faster until the people inside became a blur and the train entered the tunnel and was gone from sight.

I asked her again. "Mom, who was that lady waving at us?" It was then that she answered my question. "That was Fanny. She took care of you when you were a baby."

"Fanny," I repeated. In my mind it sounded like Nanny, the name all of the nieces and nephews called my mother. The train had pulled away from the station, leaving an empty platform. Not a single person remained, just a solitary green bench and billboards with ads for Camel cigarettes, and Coca cola. The two of us stood on the opposite side of the station saying nothing, looking back toward a train that was gone.

I felt a rush, a sudden memory opening within me. The arms that waved in synchronicity were those arms I had tried to remember, arms that held me, warmed me, loved me.

"Fanny," I said to myself. I had never heard my mother speak of Fanny before. Yet the memory of someone there, someone loving, at least in the beginning, had persisted. I had thought I'd imagined those loving feelings, thought I had dreamed her. I thought she was the aching in my heart.

"I remember her," I said.

"Oh, you were just a baby, I don't think so." My mother looked off into the distance, dismissing my comment and not looking at my upturned, interested face.

Now I asked all the questions I had never been able to ask before. I wanted to know everything. Fanny existed. And as secretive as she normally was, my mother filled me in on a few of the missing pieces of the puzzle.

My father was a postal employee who worked his way up from the Railway Mail Service where he sorted the mail on a train that ran to and from Boston from New York, to supervising the block-long mail room in the basement of the New York City Post Office. This was as high a position as he would be able to attain. The positions in the upstairs offices, all the administrative, and prestigious, high-paying jobs were withheld from Jews, no matter how impressive their work record. It was common knowledge that if you were a Jew, you could only go so far, and never upstairs. If you were black, or brown or any person of color, you couldn't even get that far. You couldn't be in charge of anything or anyone. You could only stand on your feet all day sorting and throwing the mail or doing mail delivery.

After the Depression years, those in stable government

positions who had been provided ongoing salaries during the difficult years emerged without financial loss or devastation. With services and commodities still dirt cheap and everyone recovering from the Depression, we could suddenly afford new things. So that was when my family had a baby (me), a house (our first and only home), a Chevrolet (our only car ever), and even a maid. Fanny, my mother explained, was shipped to New York from South Carolina along with many other young "colored" girls who needed jobs and could be hired out as maids and nannies to families who profited from the Depression. I had never realized the Great Depression had been good for anyone. But I guess it had. We never had money before that or much after things got back to normal.

"So what happened to her?" I asked. "Why did she go away?"

My mother took a deep breath and paused before she said, "Well, she got sick."

"Sick? What kind of sick?" I asked.

"She got a venereal disease. We took her to Dr. Edelstein." He was the family doctor who had delivered me. "He gave her some medicine and told us privately, 'Get rid of her.'"

"And so we did," she said with a sadness in her voice, a finality.

I said, "Oh," as if I understood. I knew about venereal disease; I'd heard of syphilis. But I never would understand how they could get rid of her. That's what people said about unwanted puppies. How could they get rid of this woman who loved and cared for me? What would I have given to be able to touch her, hug her, tell her I remembered her, never forgot her, because she had loved me. If we hadn't seen her on the subway station, I never would have known about Fanny, except in my dreams. Of course I never saw her again. But now I remembered.

I had a Nanny.

Last Conversation with my Mother

ON WEDNESDAY NIGHTS IN the summertime, my best friend Lyn and I took the Brooklyn/Manhattan Transit (BMT) train to Prospect Park to square dance under the stars. We were seventeen and in the fall would be seniors at Lincoln High School. I remember the night in August when I left home wearing a wildly colorful cotton skirt with yellow, green and red stripes that swirled when I did the turns, with an off-the-shoulder white eyelet cotton blouse that showed off my suntanned shoulders.

My friend also wore a peasant style blouse and lively full skirt. We dressed alike. Lyn was nine inches shorter than me and with her thick auburn hair streaming over her shoulders and my blonde hair cascading down my back, she and I looked like tall and short versions of each other. We went to the park because they offered free square-dancing with a caller and live fiddlers. We held out our flared skirts and pranced, skipped and bowed to each other and to our corners, following the instructions from the caller. We didn't go to the park to pick up boys. We loved to dance.

It was a late August night with a bright full moon and a cool breeze, a reminder that summer was nearly over. Lyn and I strolled away from the dance pavilion, munching on hot dogs smothered in mustard, and feeling the balmy Indian summer breeze. A boy—

no, a man, or what we liked to call a boy/man—turned and looked at me with a grin, stopped walking with his friend and said, "Hello."

Something about him caught me by surprise. He didn't look like the pasty-faced bland high school boys I knew. He was sultry, dark-skinned, with dark eyes and brows: He was my height, about 5'10, and older; I guessed about twenty. He introduced himself as Jeff Yabroudy. He added that he was from Syria. He had no accent. I thought he was exotic and sexy.

He trailed after us as we strolled around the park that night and at the last minute asked me for my phone number just as we were leaving to catch our train back home. I talked non-stop from the minute the train left the station at Prospect Park until it came to our stop at Sheepshead Bay and we got off. I couldn't stop my breathless chatter, about the night, about Jeff, about how I would finally date someone I liked. And about all the signs that he liked me. He followed us, he chose me, he had my phone number; he would call me.

Lyn caught her bus home to Plum Beach, a nearby neighborhood. I was so excited that I ran all the way home from the station, dashed up the stairs of our house and even though it was eleven o'clock and my parents had gone to bed, I charged into their bedroom and hopped onto my mom's side of the bed, waking her up. I couldn't wait to share my news. I had met someone I liked, for the first time ever.

I had dated a few boys when I was sixteen, but no one special, no one that took my breath away, till now. Most of them were boring. My mom sat up in her bed in her flannel nightgown and put the bedside lamp on to see what I looked like. My father continued to snore facing the other way. Nothing ever awakened him.

"I met a boy in the park," I told her excitedly. "And I like him." These were words I had never uttered. I wanted to jump up and down. I was so happy, I hugged her. This was an amazing night. I looked at her face. She was not smiling. She leaned toward me with a disapproving frown I didn't understand.

"What's wrong?" I asked.

"You picked up someone in the park?"

"No," I corrected her. "I met someone. And I really like him."

"And I suppose he's not Jewish," she stated.

Why would she say that? I hadn't even thought about that. Did it matter? Was that important?

"He's an Arab," I said, realizing this was not going well.

"Oh, my god," she said, lying back on the bed, her light brown hair spilling onto the pillow. "Well, you can't see him again." Having said this, she rolled onto her side as if she was going back to sleep and I was dismissed. The deep frown remained between her eyes as she closed them. The conversation was over.

I stood there for a moment in shock. This was the same woman who always said that I could tell her anything, and that she was my "friend." I didn't expect this. I ran out of the room and down the hall into my own small bedroom at the other end of the house. I slammed the door and threw myself on my bed. I didn't cry. I was too stunned.

I lay there staring at my mother's ugly snarly, spiny plants that lined the window sill. That was the moment that I realized my mother was not my friend and never would be. That was the moment that I decided I would never tell her anything else again, that I could never trust her with my feelings. Now I stood up and deliberately crossed to the window. With both hands I shoved the heavy window upward. Without hesitation, I picked up the tallest of the planters in its blue ceramic pot that was always in my way when I wanted to use the phone on the bedside table in front of the window. She stored her plants on the window sill even though they never flowered. They were ugly, grotesque, groping plants. It was her taste, not mine. I liked flowery plants, not these with broad prickly cactus-like protrusions, like intrusions in my bedroom.

I pried out the bottom of the screen and lifted the plant up and out the 2nd story window. I dropped it into the cement alley below.

The crash of the ceramic pot was loud. She came into my room. "What did you do?" she said seeing the window open and the plant gone. I didn't answer her. She knew. And then she showed her true colors. "You're a murderer," she said. "You kill things."

I knew I had wounded her. I had wanted to throw her out of the window. Instead I killed her plant.

After that, I sneaked out of the house evenings to meet Jeff on the street corner. I said I was going to a friend's house. But rebellion doesn't usually work. And it didn't work for me. I was always kind of in love with him but never happy when I was with him. In fact, I felt like a criminal. It was doomed. I still needed my mother's approval. Perhaps I always would need it. She had ruined this for me.

I discovered in the next five years that she would not approve of anyone I liked. So it wasn't a matter of ethnicity, or religion. She very much liked Bud, a nice, quiet (yes, Jewish) boy who wore thick glasses and stuttered. I really wasn't attracted to him but it seemed she was. She would invite him over when I was still at school and offer him homemade streudel cake and I'd come home and find them sitting at the kitchen table together talking and eating. My face dropped when I saw him there and he looked hurt and left.

"Why," I asked my mother, "did you bring him here?"

"Oh, he's so sweet, and he really likes you."

"But, Mom, I don't like him."

There were a few fellows who put color in my face when they entered the living room to pick me up. These she didn't approve of for one reason or another, even if they were Jewish. And then there was Alan who wanted to marry me. He came from a wealthy family and offered me a large rock of a diamond ring that was a family heirloom. I went out with him for about a year just to have someone to date, but I saw no future with him. He did not take my breath away. My brother called him sarcastically "Al honey" after a radio program, "My Friend Irma," about a dumb blonde with a misfit boyfriend who Irma called "Al honey."

I told Alan I couldn't take the ring if it had strings attached, which of course it did. When I told my mother, she nearly fainted with happiness.

"You'll never have to work for the rest of your life."

"Mom, I don't love him."

"You can learn to love him."

"Okay, you marry him if you like him so much," I said.

She threw her arms up in the air as if I was the unreasonable one. I left the room thinking, she'll never understand me.

AFTER COLLEGE I KNEW I had to leave home as soon as I could figure out where to go. My cousin Ellen came to New York the summer I graduated. Her mother had died in Florida and she flew to New York for the funeral. It was my mother's older sister, my Aunt Laura.

This was a cousin ten years older who I had always thought was glamorous, and pretty. She said, "Come visit me, I'm so lonely without Mom to take care of."

"You mean it?" I asked. My mind raced with the idea that I could get out of that house.

One month later I packed all my summer clothes to go visit

Ellen in Florida. I arranged deliberately to have some friends drive me to the airport so I didn't have to have my parents take me in my dad's car. As the car pulled away from the curb, with four of my college friends packed into it, I looked up at the 2nd story window and was stunned to see my mother's face framed in the window, staring down with the saddest expression I'd ever seen on it. She waved goodbye. I knew I was never coming back. I think she knew it also. But, my mother was not my friend.

Thank god I still had my brother.

My Mother is Dying

THE OLD WOMAN IN the bed was not the beautiful mother I had known. Her face was deeply lined with wrinkles, and without her dentures, her chin receded and sagged. Her gray hair had turned white since I had seen her a year ago. Her face was ashen.

She lay in a hospital bed in her own bedroom, hooked up to oxygen, a cup of water and an apple juice box next to the bed with bent straws ready for sipping.

"Hi, Mom," I said cheerfully.

She smiled and lifted her head. "Oh—Marian. You're here."

Yes, I just got in," I said, and then my mind went blank. What do you say to a mother who is dying? What is the protocol for this? It was my first experience with a dying person, let alone my mother.

I put my tote bag on the floor and sat on the edge of her bed. I noticed the faint smell of alcohol that reminded me unpleasantly of a sick room or hospital. Her small bedroom looked the same, the familiar peach-colored walls, the benign paintings of country scenes and the sliding glass doors opening to a tiny balcony enclosed with screens to keep the bugs out. Looking through the glass I noticed the patio plants looked caked and dry. Were her plants dying, too? She couldn't tend to them and without her nurturing, they couldn't survive.

The highlight of the room was the gilded, ornately framed photo of the three sisters: Laura, the ten-year-old standing behind a loveseat where three-year-old baby Estelle, and my mother Roselle, about seven at the time of the photo, sat unsmiling. Roselle's arm was around her baby sister. The two older girls wore white sailor blouses with ties and long navy skirts. The baby wore a pale pink dress with white stockings and high backed shoes.

The photo, touched up to look like a painting, with pink highlight in the girls' cheeks, and faded blue in the love-seat, was somber. No one was smiling. Maybe that was the style for photographs in the 1920's. I remember all the deadly wedding portraits: bride standing behind seated groom, her hand on his shoulder, rather grim, no romance here. This was a serious portrait of my mother and my two aunts looking at the camera with no expression.

My mother was now the only living member of this family. I stared at the photo. I thought, what a pretty little girl my mother had been, an unimaginable degeneration to this shriveled being in the bed.

"How are you feeling?" I stupidly asked. She looked like hell.

"So-so," she answered. Her speech lisped without her teeth.

"What can I get you?" I asked, not having a clue of what I could do for her. She shrugged. "I don't know." Her breath smelled of decay. I felt sick seeing her like this.

My brother and his wife lived in Del Rey Beach, Florida, not far from my parents in West Palm Beach, and were able to see them frequently. Rob, always the good son, took on the responsibility of taking care of them. Living in Los Angeles, no doubt as far away as I could get, I visited my parents once or twice a year and dreaded those occasions. They still treated me as the defective child, even speaking of me in the third person. "Do you think she'll want to eat at six? What time should we pick her up?" And I was right there in the car with them! In their presence I became seven years old again, helpless and angry.

When I got the call from my brother, I was trying to stay calm and recover from a killer work assignment. As a School Psychologist in Los Angeles Schools, I had a good reputation for competent and quality work. I was well liked, personally and professionally. My reward for twenty years of hard work was an assignment to serve five chaotic schools per week. The stress of trying to get the avalanche of cases done, attend meetings, assess students, counsel the kids, teachers and families, and deal with crises and demanding administrators gave me splitting headaches. The migraines finally landed me at Kaiser Emergency to see a neurologist who tested for brain tumors.

Everything was negative when he announced, "I've seen this before. It's called an LAUSD headache."

I said, "Really?"

He recommended a stress leave. I had never heard of that but grabbed it gratefully.

"Yes, get me out of there," I said. The job was making me crazy. The leave turned into a workman's comp case and I was required to see a psych weekly. He wasn't very good and often fell asleep during our sessions, saying he was just closing his eyes.

I knew he was sleeping. "Am I boring you?" I asked. He was of no help to me except to pump up the case and show I was in treatment.

I planned to take an early retirement in June and then face the inevitable trip to visit my parents. I hated Florida. Miami was where David left me (the first time) and where I married on the rebound and had a child. I had allergies to the mold and fungus that thrived in the humid climate and gave me asthma attacks. I lived on cortisone with an oxygen tent in the bedroom. I ran away from all of it and swore I'd never go there again.

But my parents moved there after my father retired. Why did they have to choose Florida? I visited them mostly out of guilt. My brother was always on the scene being the good son. I was still the bad girl.

The minute I got off the plane, I felt congested and out of breath. Oh yes, I hated Florida for many reasons. But here I was, like it or not.

It was April when I got the call from Rob. "Mom's worse. Maybe you should come out now and not wait till summer."

By now we all knew she had lung cancer. No way to avoid this, I flew out right away. At the airport, he tried to prepare me.

"Brace yourself," he said. "I don't think you'll recognize her. She got old." I knew she was 90. But I never expected this.

"Would you like some ice cream?" I asked her. Mom used to serve "black and white" ice cream sodas at nine o'clock every night. In all the years I lived in that house in Sheepshead Bay, I can't recall her ever missing a night. She'd hand them out in the living room as we watched TV. My father, in his recliner, was given his soda first. Then my brother and I got ours. They were the best I've ever had. We tried to make them as good, but never succeeded, something in the way she knew just how much Hershey's chocolate syrup, and just how much seltzer, and topping it off with the right amount of milk and vanilla ice cream. It was her secret formula, never to be duplicated in her life time.

I knew there'd be some ice cream in her freezer.

"All right," she said agreeably. I put some strawberry ice cream in a dish, propped her head up on pillows and fed her a teaspoon at a time. I wiped the dribbles off her chin with a towel near the bed. This was an odd feeling. She had always been pushing food into me and now I was feeding her. What a reversal.

I tried to comb her short white hair. I had never done that in my life. She seemed to like my touching her and smiled. I had avoided this for years. It felt too risky to show affection to her. But looking at her now, helpless and decrepit, she didn't scare me anymore. She couldn't send me away for being a bad child. She was a dying woman, not a powerful force.

The doctors said she had terminal lung cancer. Her lungs were shot. I remembered the numerous times I asked her on the phone how she was and she complained about coughing. I was an asthmatic. I knew about breathing problems. We had something in common.

When I visited her a year ago, she told me again, "Dad and Robert don't think I cough that much. They don't believe me." I immediately thought of my father smoking cigars and pipes for all of the years of their marriage. I remember they argued about it and recently she made him smoke outside on the balcony. But it was too late. She had breathed in secondhand smoke for sixty years.

I went through the yellow pages to call and compare prices from three steam cleaning companies. "Dad, it's the smoke that's making Mom cough," I argued. "We need to get the drapes and carpets cleaned."

I told my brother the same thing. Rob said, "Oh, when she's busy, she forgets to cough. I don't think it's anything serious." He was discrediting her. I knew what that felt like too. I was furious and determined to get the place cleaned. My mother surprised me when she said, "You're the only one who believes me." This was the first time she had turned to me for help. She had been my care-giver when I was sick. I thought how awful to be old and sick and dependent on the people around you, and not heard. I had spent my entire childhood feeling that no one heard me. I understood this. The same smoke that had given me asthma when I was thirteen was killing my mother.

That week I stayed at a Day's Inn nearby since there was no space for me in their small apartment. This was actually a gift. My dad had hired a Jamaican caregiver named Dorothy who slept on the living room pull-out sofa, while he shared the bedroom with my mom. I watched him as he hovered around my mother. I had never seen him treat her with such tenderness. They had always argued about everything. If she said black, he said white. "You're wrong, Herman," she would say. I called it "bicker and dicker."

Now he touched her head and said gently, "How's my little girl?"

I thought, "he knows she's dying." I couldn't believe he called her his little girl. He was 95, and she was 90. I had never seen this side of him. It dawned on me that he loved her. I had never noticed affection between them. Amazing!

I sat by her bedside every day, from early morning till after dark. I fed her ice cream and sang to her all the songs of my childhood, songs that she taught me. I sang the first song I ever learned. She inhaled and sighed aloud when I began. I remembered every word in the lyric.

> Shine your shoes, Brush your hair, Come along with me.
> It's Mickey Mouse's Birthday Party, that's the place to be.
> The 3 little pigs and the big bad wolf are playing piggy back.
> There's Minnie dressed in her Sunday best,
> and Donald Duck with his quack, quack, quack quack.

And back to the verse. I held her hand as I sang this child's song.

> Ring those bells, Toot those horns, Let the world be gay.
> It's Mickey Mouse's Birthday Party, What a holiday!

When I finished, she tried to laugh, and coughed instead. But she was pleased. Our special song was *Till We Meet Again*. I would sing the lead part, while she harmonized in her light falsetto soprano, just over the melody. The same thing always happened. I tried as hard as I could to stay on the tune, but inevitably ended up joining her and singing the harmony. We would stop singing, look at each other and laugh. Always the same. I never could stay on key. I would fall off. I think I always wanted to be in harmony with her—in our lives as in our singing. But I always fell off the notes in trying so hard.

My nights in the motel were sleepless. I tried to read but couldn't concentrate. My eyes read the same line over and over without any comprehension of the meaning. I watched television, but there was nothing on the screen that interested me, just an old movie, some infomercials, a blank screen. Finally I turned off the TV around 3:00 a.m. and tried to sleep. I listened to the road noises outside, an occasional door slamming, a baby crying in another room. I wanted to see my friends. I missed my cats. I wanted to go home.

The light finally peeked around the closed edges of the motel drapes and I was relieved to know it was daylight. I was not a morning person. But I needed to get over to see her. I was trying to be a good daughter. It was my last chance. I knew I had never been a good child. It was my mother who reminded me of that. Maybe I could be good now.

I got up at six, ate an over-ripe banana I had stored in the tiny ice-box, put on shorts and a tee shirt, sandals and a hat and walked three blocks to my parents' co-op apartment. It was already getting hot and humid, and my skin was wet when I walked into the sick room. Another day with my dying mother.

A week later, I sat on the edge of her bed, wondering how to say goodbye. I said, "Mom, is it okay if I go home tomorrow?" I felt weary and in need of sleep.

She said, "I'm going home too," as she closed her eyes.

The hair on my arms stood straight up. She knew. I had heard people speak of "going home" before they died. I didn't believe they actually used those words.

My brother arrived later, and as we stood in the kitchen together, I told him what she had said. "It doesn't mean what you think it means," he insisted.

Dorothy, her caregiver, heard me and said quietly, "Yes, she's going home soon," I put my arms around Dorothy and held her.

Back in my mom's room, I sat in a chair watching her sleep. Her breath was raspy, an awful sound. I confirmed my reservation on Delta Airlines to leave the next morning. It would be a full day's trip home. I'd probably never see her again. There was something I needed to say, something important. It felt urgent. As if she knew, her eyes flickered open. I held back, not ready to risk yet.

Instead I said, "Mom, let's sing our song." She nodded. Her eyes watched me for her cue. Will she be able to sing? I wondered.

I began. "*Smile the while I kiss you sad adieu.*"

She tried to join me. Her voice was frail and faint. If I leaned my ear toward her mouth and listened, I could hear the thin thread of harmony. I continued singing. The room was quiet. My father, brother, sister-in-law and Dorothy waited in the living room to give us this time together. I knew they were listening. I continued singing.

"*When the clouds roll by, I'll come to you....*"

Her soprano voice was soft and almost inaudible, but she was singing. I was leading her this time.

"*Then the skies will seem more blue,*
Down in lover's lane my dearie,
Wedding bells will ring so merrily,

Every tear will be a memory.
So wait and pray each night for me,
Till we meet again."

The last two lines caught in my throat. I choked on the words. Will we meet again? I thought, no, I will never see my mother again. This is the last time we will sing together. I had stayed on key and didn't lose the melody because she was too weak to throw me off.

It was time to tell her. The words were waiting. Would she remember? And more than that—would she give me what I needed from her?

The most important words I ever said to my mother were,

"Mommy, can I have a puppy? Please, Mommy, I'll take care of it, I promise." I took a deep breath. Yes, I would ask her again. It was now or never.

Like the final request of a dying man, I reached for hope. Can you, my mother, know who I am? Can you understand my longings, my passions, my dreams? Can I ask you to approve of me now that it's almost over? And in a flash I knew this was the moment. There would be no other. I blurted it out.

"Mom, I'm getting a puppy."

She tried to lift her head from the pillow. I watched her face for a reaction. This was important. I had to lean in to hear her words.

"You always wanted a dog," she whispered.

She remembered.

And that should have been enough. She asked, "What are you going to call it?" I was amazed she even cared—this mother who hated animals was asking me what I was going to name the dog I'd wanted all my life, the dog she had denied me, someone who could love and acknowledge me in ways I was never loved or acknowledged by her. This mother who told me I was a bad child, who made me feel undeserving of anything, wanted to know about my puppy.

"Holly Go Lightly," I answered hopefully. I nearly stopped breathing in anticipation of what she would think of this, so "un-Jewish" a name. I actually wanted her to like my choice. Wasn't it enough she remembered about the puppy? I wanted more.

I waited. There was a long pause. "Do you like it?" I broke the silence. I needed to know. Please like it, I thought. Please like my choices. Please like me.

I heard water running in the next room. Someone was washing the dishes.

My ninety-year-old mother lifted her head to inform me,

"I don't have to like it. Only you do."

I sighed, resigned. Don't ask for too much, I thought. I had hoped that she would finally approve of my life, of my dreams and hopes and passions, that she would be happy for me. I really needed her blessing. I was amazed she even remembered that I wanted a puppy. But her approval? Why do I still need it? Nothing had changed.

It was a long trip home to Culver City with connecting flights from West Palm Beach to Dallas to LAX that took more than ten hours with the lay-over. Half way home I was dragging my luggage through the mammoth Dallas airport when I felt a sudden urge to call her. Tears filled my eyes. I stopped walking and looked around for a phone. There was none. I boarded my plane to L.A. without making the call.

Slowly climbing the stairs inside my condo, I dragged my heavy carry-on bag behind me. I was beyond tired. The phone was ringing and I knew who it was. I let it ring while I made my way through the living room, down the hall and into my bedroom. My three cats were sprawled out on my bed waiting for me to return, burrowing into my unmade and rumpled bed where my scent was heaviest. The lamp beside the bed was lit and the radio played classical music. I tried to keep life in the house even though I had a pet sitter who came by twice a day.

My brother's voice: "Marian—Mom died—right after you left." He faltered and waited through the silence as I sucked in my breath and lowered myself onto the bed.

"So I'm afraid you're going to have to come back," he finished. And waited.

I couldn't believe he would ask me to get on two planes tomorrow and do it all again—for a funeral—not for my mother. She was no longer there. Why would I do this?

"I can't," I said in a desperate voice, reaching out for Samantha, my smallest cat, my hand moving from her sweet head down her grey furry back. She felt warm to my touch and fell over on her back, stretching out sensuously on my pillow. Another silence.

"I'm not coming back," I said feeling more definite. "I'm exhausted."

He was silent.

I asked, "Rob—Do you need me? I'll come for you."

He said, "No, I have Bernice, and the kids. You don't need to come for me."

"I'll be sick if I have to do it again."

"If you get sick, I'll just have to come out and take care of you," he said. Yes, he still was in charge of taking care of his kid sister. Nothing had changed. We were all as we had been.

Finally he asked, "What will I tell them when they ask where you are?"

This was the wrong question. Why couldn't he have asked me how I felt about Mom? Why couldn't he have shared his grief with me? Why couldn't he have spoken of the pain of our lives? Who cared what people would think? I lay back and looked up at the ceiling fan spinning so fast I couldn't distinguish one blade from another.

"Tell them I already said goodbye to Mom."

In the morning I called my father.

"Dad, do you need me to come back? I'll come for you."

"Marian—just take care of yourself. I'm all right." He had never given me permission to care about myself. He sounded loving. Something *had* changed.

I didn't go to the funeral, I had said all the goodbyes that I had within me. There were no more. I wrote down the lyrics of our song and sent the song with my daughter Terrie, the Nanny's grandchild to read at the funeral service. From me to my mom.

I never knew if she sang or spoke the words, but the song was there to say my final goodbye, our song. So *wait and pray each night for me—Till We Meet Again.*

On the day of the funeral I sat on my patio with a few close friends. My best friend Lyn brought a platter of food from the deli. It was just like her to think of this. Sally brought flowers, as beautiful as her soft words. I spoke to my dad on the phone. He really was okay. He actually sounded concerned about me.

Lyn called the next day to see how I was feeling.

"I'm fine," I said.

"You're fine?" she said, surprised. "You can't be over this so quickly. Your mother just died."

I sighed deeply. "I lost her a long time ago."

PART II

THE MEN

Coney Island Memoirs

ON SATURDAYS, MY BROTHER and I were sent out for the day. Sometimes this meant going to our neighborhood movie theatre, the Sheepshead, to see The Three Stooges, Perils of Pauline, Chaplin comedies, cartoons, a newsreel and a double feature of two movies. That kept us busy and out of the house for the day. My parents gave little or no thought to the content of the films we saw and I had many nightmares about the Wolfman and Frankenstein monsters. In the theater, I would pull my sweater over my head and try not to look. At home I was often afraid to go into a dark room for fear a monster would jump out and get me.

Other Saturdays we took the trolley car to Steeple Chase, an amusement park in Coney Island, named for the famed horse racing track of the same name. At the entrance to the park stood a giant statue of the symbolic horse and jockey. As we approached, what we saw from the streetcar was the tallest roller coaster ride in the world, "The Cyclone." Only the very brave or stupid went on this ride; it was a status symbol to say that you rode the dreaded Cyclone. Neither my brother nor I were ever foolish or brave enough to get on it. The first drop appeared to fall right into the Atlantic Ocean, and then pull out into a very sharp curve at the last second. We could hear the screams miles away.

We walked around Coney Island for free and ate those golden brown bubbling hot dogs at Nathan's for five cents each. We floated around the boardwalk, went into the penny arcades with just a penny each, and poked our heads through visual funnels to watch rapidly moving cards simulating silent movies; Chaplin, Our Gang, Buster Keaton, and even some nude women in various exotic poses and moves in what they called the dirty penny arcades. So I knew why the men went in there.

But the Steeple Chase was like a private club. It cost a whole dime; and this was a commitment for the afternoon that entitled you to go on all the rides, and see everything, and I do mean everything. Going into the place was scary to me. The only way in was to cross a stage in front of an audience seated there to laugh at you. First you encountered the bumpy moving floor; with everyone trying to keep their balance, and some falling, and the audience laughing and cat-calling. There were gigantic barrels turning that you had to crawl through to get into the place. It was like a test to see if you could pass the first obstacle course. Then the clowns appeared with the wands that blew air up the women's dresses as they came across the moving floor; and the women screamed and tried to hold their dresses down. This was of course before women were allowed to wear slacks in public. There was something sexual about that for me as a seven-year-old; watching the reaction of the men in the audience to women's dresses way up over their heads; in their bloomers, and occasionally wearing no underpants at all. The audience howled; and the lascivious midget clowns looked like evil dwarfs doing mischief so perverted that it elicited my first memory of sexual feelings, so strong, that I masturbated on the trolley going home. I just squeezed my legs together, with my brother sitting right there on the seat next to me. And after that I had a visual to elicit the same feelings. It was of those naughty little grinning men with their blower wands, something about their smirks as they embarrassed women by looking under their dresses that was erotic to me even as a child.

The rides: sooh frightening; Rob, too busy taking care of me to be scared, he said later. Me: terrified, and clinging to him, begging him to end the ride. "Make it stop." But he couldn't. My terror on the rides I was forced into reflected my general state of anxiety, with feelings of nausea, and dizziness thrown in as a bonus. Yet still we went. Today diagnosed with vestibular migraine manifesting in chronic motion sickness brings awareness of the early onset of this condition. I didn't know I was allowed to say no. I probably wasn't, or what could ever have stopped me from screaming "no" like a rape victim. The theme of my life. I didn't know I was allowed to say no. I'm just discovering that freedom now, and only some of the time. I don't know why we had to do this. I wondered for years later if my brother thought he was supposed to take me on the rides, and that he wasn't allowed to say no either. I never asked him, so I don't really know. Wouldn't it be something if he hated it also. So he took me on circular rides, round cars that turned in circles, parachute jumps, roller coasters, and the least lethal, the drive your own car, where, he recklessly bumped as many cars as he could. I felt bruised and shaken when I got out, and never thought it was much fun. The only thing that I showed real interest in were the house of mirrors. I got to see myself fatter. Since I was close to skeletal from not eating the food in my mother, the food pusher's kitchen; seeing myself filled out, and looking better was a miracle of sorts. I just looked and looked, until he came and pulled me away to continue my torture on yet another ride.

The Magical World of Suicide

When I was 18 I decided to kill myself. There was a way out.

On the day of my graduation from Abraham Lincoln High School, I wore a lilac-colored dress with matching jacket with a corsage of one fragrant gardenia pinned to it. The color of my outfit paid homage to my newly found purple phase. It also complied with the directive to dress for the commencement in pale floral shades. Lyn wore lime green, also linen, with a prim buttoned jacket. It looked great with her long flaming auburn hair. She and I were wallflowers. We didn't seem to fit in with the cute popular girls who wore cashmere sweaters, and hung out in cliques and went steady. We found each other because we felt like outcasts. We were an odd couple; I was 5'10", she only five feet.

"Hey, daddy longlegs," said the high school boys, inches shorter than me. "What basketball team do you play for?" Not one boy ever asked me out on a date. When we were seen together, they called us Mutt and Jeff. Completely unpopular, we depended on each other for company and laughter. It was she who introduced me to the joy of eating. I had the first fun meal of my life with her.

After school, we often stopped at a neighborhood pizza parlor. There was definitely no pizza in my mother's kitchen.

I couldn't believe that food could taste good and be fun to eat. In the pizza parlor with Lyn, no one said, "Eat, you must eat." No one made me sit alone at the table till bedtime, or watch intensely every bite I tried to force into my mouth. The long strings of cheese dripping off the slices landed on my blouse and left grease spots. My friend and I laughed. I ate. I think she saved my life.

After the graduation ceremony, my parents took my brother and me to Prospect Park to take pictures to mark the occasion. We went out for dinner to a Chinese restaurant. I was able to eat the chicken chow mein, egg roll, won ton soup and ice cream. It was only in my kitchen with my mother that I lost my appetite. However, eating Chinese food with my father was an embarrassment because he called the waiters "Charlie." They didn't seem to mind and came to the table smiling as if it wasn't derogatory. But my brother and I thought he was racist. All auto mechanics were "Mac" in a similar display of stereotypes. Truck drivers were "Joe."

Growing up poor on the East side of New York may have had something to do with these vernaculars. My Dad had no education beyond 6th grade when he had to drop out of school and go to work in the family grocery store. His poor grammar—"oil" pronounced 'erl' and other butchering of language—was another embarrassment to me. I wanted him to speak correctly. No wonder he didn't want to send me to college. I might become smarter than he was, and for a girl, that wouldn't be right, since he didn't even go to high school.

So I didn't think it was strange that no time during that day or night did anyone discuss my future plans. Go to college? Get a job? Kill myself? My parents never seemed to have any expectations for me. Girls didn't need educations. And besides that, I was defective, so why bother.

I had no idea what I was supposed to do. I guessed that they expected me to get married. College was not an option, no more than Hebrew school or going to sporting events, or being allowed out of the house independently had been. Many of the girls graduating in my class were going steady or engaged. I didn't even go to the prom. If not for my one good friend, I was pretty much a loner.

I didn't dare dream of the luxury of going away to college. My family had no money for that. My brother had already graduated and was working on his Master's. It was understood that he would get an education. He was a boy. He was sent to Hebrew School. He was the important child. He had to earn a living, support a family. Everyone expected him to graduate from college. And he did.

There were no goals for me. I made the decision to go to Brooklyn College, tuition free, and live at home because I didn't know what else to do. This meant I would be living with my family for another four years, an eternity of hell. But what were the choices? I had to do something, be somewhere. So I did what he did. And they didn't seem to care, though my father opposed it openly. "Girls don't need an education," he said. "What do they need it for? They're gonna get married and have kids." I wondered who I was. I seemed suited for nothing.

It was week one. My knees shook as I sat in the first classroom clutching a small lined pad to write down all of the assignments and requirements for the semester. It was English 1. The bearded instructor stood in the front of the room, arms folded across his chest, laying it all out in a monotone voice.

"This is Brooklyn College," he said. "The easy just get-by days of high school are over." His appearance and lack of warmth scared me. "Here you will be expected to meet high standards, turn in assignments, write papers, take the regular exams or flunk out."

By now I was in a cold sweat. I feared I would drown in papers and tests and more failures. I moved robotically from class to class that day and through the week. Math 1, Spanish 1, Bio1, my assignment pad growing thicker and more scribbly. Leaving each classroom and wandering around the enormous campus, I felt desperate. I was not going to succeed at this. By the end of the first week I had met with all my instructors and had heard all of the impossible tasks I was being asked to accomplish. I knew I would fail. Things looked bleak.

At home, I shared none of my concerns with my family. They didn't really care. I closed the bedroom door and picked up the phone. When I was scared I called my best friend to whom I told everything.

"Lyn—I'm going to kill myself," I said calmly. "I'm going to jump in the bay." I was referring to Sheepshead Bay, an outlet to the Atlantic Ocean and the name of my neighborhood. The solution to my problems was a mere block away from my house and I could walk there. My friend, in her typically accepting way said, "Okay—but could you wait a little while?"

I agreed to wait. In less than a half hour Lyn appeared at the top of the stairs, out of breath. She had run all the way from her house in Plum Beach, about a 20 minute run. She said cheerfully, "There's a new Martin and Lewis movie at the Sheepshead theatre. Wanna' go?"

We loved Dean Martin and Jerry Lewis movies, and usually laughed until we fell on the floor. We saw *Sailor Beware* and in the scene where they are sent out to swab the deck of the submarine, and it starts to submerge, we started laughing the way we always laughed together. We roared. In the middle of that contagious hysteria, Lyn poked me in the ribs with her elbow. I looked over at her.

"You're going to kill yourself?" she said.

I smiled and said, "Oh," understanding that life still was worth living. I think she saved me from the bay many times.

Suicide had its own glamour and magic for me. Jumping into Sheepshead Bay sounded dramatic. How else does one do it? Pills? Guns? I didn't have access to anything else, just the cold waters of the bay. I was drowning anyway. My father had tossed me into the Atlantic Ocean when I was little in order to teach me to swim. I knew what drowning felt like on many levels.

I often fantasized my own funeral. I had sworn Lyn to promise that she'd hire the makeup artist of the movie stars, Wally Westmore, to make up my face to be sure I'd be beautiful. She promised she would. In my fantasy, I would lie in an open coffin, as lovely and peaceful as Sleeping Beauty, or Snow White, and all the people in my life would form a circle around the coffin, and feel sorry about their behavior toward me while I was alive. All those who had hurt me, been mean to me, didn't understand me would be there. And they would all look at me lovingly. And they would all suffer regret. How could we have treated her so terribly? How could we have not seen the pain, the unhappiness? Why didn't we know? And they would all love me now that I'm dead.

My mother used to say, "You'll be sorry when I'm gone." I teased, "Where are you going, Ma? When are you leaving?" I never took her seriously. Mothers don't leave. They stay with us forever. It is we who must leave them. But the line, "You'll be sorry..." resonated with me, except the words I used were, "They'll be sorry when I'm gone."

They'll be sorry when I'm gone. They'll be sorry they didn't hear me. They'll be sorry they were so mean to me. And best one of all, "They'll be sorry they didn't know how much I was suffering." It was pointless to kill myself unless it taught them a lesson, unless it made them love me. I wouldn't want to fail at suicide too.

A Room of my Own

I NEVER IMAGINED HE'D leave me with "them." When my brother announced that he was getting married, I was devastated. He was the only one in the house who seemed to understand me. It was his bed I crawled into at night when I was afraid of the monster shadows on the walls of my little room, and it was his voice that helped me get to sleep.

"Whenever you feel scared of anything, just picture yourself the next day when it's over," he would say. And that's what I did. My terrors turned out to be temporary. I always recovered.

My compensation for the loss of my brother was that I inherited his bedroom, a room I had always coveted. For nineteen years I had been stored in a small dark room the size of a walk-in closet, with a window facing an alley offering stale air and a less than scenic view of a red brick wall twelve feet away. Robert's room was bright with sunshine and fresh air from the three windows that looked out over a back yard and garage. From these windows, I could watch my father fertilizing his yellow rose bushes, his purple irises, and his pride, the "Victory Garden"—a concept left over from World War II when families were encouraged to grow their own produce to be patriotic. He had the tomato plants, lettuce and string beans marked precisely with sticks holding up the identifying pictures on the seed packets. I often stood at the window watching him nurture his garden.

Besides sunshine, fresh air and a view, my brother's room had a real clothes closet. My blouses, skirts and dresses had been smashed and wrinkled from hanging on a door rack.

My sad little room had always signified to me my low ranking in this family. But then, many things reflected my status. My brother was sent away to Boy Scout camp every summer while I stayed home with the prison guards. The splendor of Sundays watching the Brooklyn Dodgers play ball at Ebbits Field or Yankee Stadium was reserved for my father's son, not for me. He was a boy, and I could never compete with that. When Rob was sent to Hebrew school, I pleaded to go too. It was just for boys who were becoming men, my father explained.

"Besides," he said, "Hebrew is much too difficult for you."

Sports were ruled out as well. When I wanted ice skates, I was told "You'll freeze to death. You'll fall down and get hurt." There was apparently nothing I could do well according to my father. I was certain that my older brother was the favored child to whom privileges were given. So I just stayed at home, watching by the window for him to come back while he was out playing stick ball in the dirt field across the street.

Now I was getting the room I wanted, and losing the brother I needed.

Before I was officially moved in, my father decided to paint the room. My dad was the painter, carpenter, plumber, electrician, gardener and decorator for our home. His taste was questionable.

I remembered when his 1939 Chevy began to rust away and he bought the wrong paint, and covered half of it using shiny enamel in a nauseating chartreuse color. My brother and I had thrown open the bedroom window of the sunny room and Rob yelled out to him, "Dad, it looks like house paint." But he was undaunted, and continued.

By the time the bottom half of the car was completed and the car came alive like a neon sign, he went back to the paint store to ask for another color of green, announcing that it was his intention to paint it two-toned, and that he didn't make a mistake. It was all planned. My father never made a mistake in his life.

So now he bought another green to contrast with the gaudy green. This one was a sort of pea green in a flat paint, and he proceeded to lather it onto the top half of the car, the entire time protesting that he wanted a two toned car. We all groaned as we watched. He painstakingly delineated between the chartreuse and the pea green so that the colors would not seep into each other and create yet another obnoxious tone. He was successful and stood proudly in the sun admiring his work as it dried, while we all grimaced, standing at the bedroom window of the room destined to be mine.

And he actually drove it, with the three of us captive. My mother was never allowed to learn how to drive: "One driver in the family is enough," he would argue whenever she asked him to teach her. I never understood that logic, but he said it was about cutting down on family mortality. Maybe so, but it also cut down on my mother's independence.

From inside the car, we could not fully appreciate the spectacle. But wherever we traveled, people all over Brooklyn recognized us. We were famous. We would find notes stuck in the windshield from people we knew and others we didn't know. Some of them said, "Hi, Herman, spotted your car a few blocks away." Strangers yelled out at us, "What carnival did that Chevy escape from?"

Even the police in Sheepshead Bay and Brighton Beach waved to us when they recognized our eyesore.

When my father asked me what color I wanted for my new bedroom, I was relieved that the choice was mine.

Every evening after midnight, I lay in bed next to my radio listening to a disc jockey named Al Collins broadcast from "The Purple Grotto." He used as an opening and closing theme, the popular love song, *Deep Purple.* " Drifting into sleep to the lyric "Lover, we'll always meet, here in my deep purple dreams" apparently had an effect on me, judging by the purple dresses, sweaters, and shawls I wore everyday.

I had not yet learned that it was the most unflattering color I could have chosen. In the world of color cosmetics reflecting the seasons, I discovered years later I was an "autumn" and should wear fall colors. Purple was draining and made me look lifeless, colorless, and Dracula-like. But at the time, I thought purple was me. Today with outrageous hair colors being flaunted, I realize I never got in touch with true rebellion.

I told him I wanted a purple room. My mother screamed. My father went right out to the paint store and searched for that color, and all by himself painted the entire room. It was exactly right. I sat in the doorway cross-legged on the floor watching the long brush strokes turn my room into the purple grotto.

My father had never given me anything I really wanted before.

While he painted, I bent over the bathtub, soaking a pair of white organdy curtains and bedspread in a violet dye to contrast with the dark walls. After the paint dried, I cut out large lavender felt letters, stood on a chair and glued them all over the walls, from one end to the other. It read, "Purple Pits of Passion." This actually got by the censors.

I loved that room; it was my last hurrah before I left my childhood home. I, too, would be escaping from this house in a few years when I graduated from Brooklyn College.

My parents may have kept it that color for a few years, but

one summer when I came to New York with my five-month-old baby, I found the purple had been covered over with a boring beige, the violet curtains had been replaced with colorless drapes, and my parents had moved into it and made it theirs. I didn't blame them. It was the largest, sunniest room in the house. All who slept there were nurtured.

NOW WHEN I MOURN the many ways in which my father damaged my perception of myself and smile over the infamous green car of my childhood, I need also to remember the purple room that he gave me—simply because I wanted it.

Be Not Afeard

I'M ON A PROP plane flying home to visit my first love. I'm 23 years old, and leaving a furnished but rather plain apartment in Miami, Florida, an apartment whose only redeeming feature was that scotch taped to the living room wall was a full-page black and white newspaper photo of my beloved. To endure the pain of separation, under the newspaper photo I had printed the words— MY GRAY CITY.

The New York Skyline symbolized my love affair with New York City, the first and most enduring love of my life. New York and I have changed through these many decades; we have aged, been hurt, abused, sullied, angered and seen destruction, yet still the magic, excitement and era of hope lives within us both, is constant and steadfast, and unshakeable. She and I have been through a lifetime of broken promises, yet still supported each other and were always connected. I know the meaning behind the lyric, "If I can make it here, I'll make it anywhere." Being from New York was my legacy.

When I was twelve years old, wearing a felt hat with dotted tulle veiling on the brim, gloves, hose and little heels, I rode on the subway alone into Manhattan from Brooklyn in a much safer world than any I have known since. When I graduated from

Brooklyn College, I faced the ache of leaving, not my family, but my city.

Although New York City is made up of five boroughs, for me it was only about Manhattan, the other boroughs were simply links to The City. You never said you were going into Manhattan for the day. You said you were going into The City, and everyone knew. New York had to be the only city in the world, or so we thought. Growing up there had given me a legacy of hope, excitement, opportunities, education, theater, ballet, opera, museums, and all of it free. Where else in the world could I have taken a train from the steps of Lincoln High School in Brooklyn, carrying school books, wearing black and white saddle shoes with bobby sox, a sweater and skirt, and commuted all the way to the top balcony of the City Center to see the greatest ballet in the world for $1.20?

Moving to Miami, designed to get me away from my family, could never compensate for what I had given up. Miami offered all year sunshine, clean beaches with warm ocean water, swimming pools, no snow, no theatre, no culture. People seemed to talk, walk and react more slowly than they did in New York. I was hungry for the stimulation and pace I had left.

The aircraft tilted as we flew over the Empire State Building, like a salute, and the skyline of my gray city, no longer gray at night, lit up, sparkled, and said, "Welcome home."

I had goose-bumps and announced to the woman sitting next to me, "This is my city." When you are from New York, you are naturally arrogant because you know you are superior.

In my first job in Miami, I came across a comment on my intake forms...it said, "New York personality." I was not offended.

Now coming home again, I was actually so stirred, so hopeful at this glorious sight that even the prospect of staying with my parents for nearly two weeks didn't seem so awful. The self-hatred and depression that they had carefully nurtured was postponed. I was coming home to my love, New York.

In my home, we were not allowed to celebrate Christmas "because you are a Jew," my mother explained. Not being sure what that meant, let alone who I was, I understood Christmas to mean a holiday, off from school, off from work, a time to watch the whole world celebrate. When the schools closed for any reason, I celebrated as well, no matter what the cause. Leaking plumbing, and a closed school building was as festive a holiday to me. My Christian friends never understood that Christmas didn't mean the same thing to me as it did to them. If I chose to work, or do something ordinary, they would say, "But it's Christmas" as if that were enough reason. And now that I was a second grade teacher and it was Christmas, I gladly took down the decorations, locked my classroom door and went home for the holidays. My parents expected me to slip right back into the defective child role and they, the competent empowered parents, were there to take care of all my shortcomings. This was our scenario, and for about a week I played the role I knew best. I spent my days in the kitchen watching my mother cook, sleeping late and hanging around the house. I was waited on like the helpless child I had been.

Then one sunny day I ventured out of the house and took a walk around the old neighborhood, I ran into Gilly Gotler who used to live across the street from us and now was home for the holidays seeing his family. I learned that he had become a successful attorney living in Cleveland. I hadn't seen him in ten years. He must have been twenty-seven now. I had never noticed him except as a kid playing stick ball in the street. And he certainly had not noticed the tall, skinny, anorexic thirteen-year-old with a bump on her nose three years before plastic surgery, and sort of geeky looking. No, he never noticed me. None of the boys did, not for the next few years, when it all changed; all except my self-concept which remained the same. Lord knows I was no longer skinny, yet still thought of myself as geeky.

But this day was different. Today this curly-headed young man who resembled the kid he had been looked at me for the first time. His eyes opened wide with surprise when he realized who I was.

"You can't be Rob's kid sister," he said.

"And you can't be Gilly," I answered.

"I'm Gil now," he explained. And then he did the most wonderful thing he could have done. He asked me out. Not just out, but for New Year's Eve. What a stroke of luck...not to have to stay home with my parents. My brother was married and gone from the house, and it would have been just *them and me.*

I said a fast yes! This boy I remembered was all grown up and he wanted to take me out on a date on New Year's Eve. I was thrilled to my toes. I tried on every stitch of clothing I'd brought with me and even the remnants of things still hanging in my old dreary little cramped closet and settled for a tight black sheath skirt with slits, and a tight black sweater with scooped out neckline. I was Hot!

When he came to the house to pick me up, my parents actually seemed pleased. This puzzled me. God, they knew him. They knew his family. My mother had played mah jong with his mother for years. Somehow they didn't try to ruin it.

I later discovered that being a Jewish attorney was a plus in their value system. A few years later, I was to marry one of these types in Florida, a nice Jewish lawyer, for my parents' sake as it turned out, certainly not for mine. The die had been cast, when I saw how happy they were with Gilly.

I emerged from the bedroom and again his eyes lit up when he looked at me. He said he couldn't get over how I'd turned out. I thought he looked okay, but wasn't concerned about what he looked like, or even who he was. Where we went was what mattered.

We were in New York, the best place in the world to be on New Year's Eve. We took the subway train into the city, and got off at Times Square, the best and most crowded spot. Even though we were cold to the bone, we walked all over the city feeling the chill of the night, but warmed by the throngs of what felt like millions of people touching, bumping, walking shoulder to shoulder with us. We stuck our heads inside every night spot, watched the circles of smoke blowing out of the Camel sign and looked up at the top of the NY Times Building which would later mark the end of 1957.

I can't ever remember feeling more alive and at the right place at the right time at the center of the world than this night. We went to a small French restaurant on 49th St. and neither one of us drank, so we remained quite sober and alert to every sight and sound. He watched me. That was what I needed. Not to like somebody but to be liked, loved, admired, and god help me, approved of. And he did all of that on this night.

We walked around after a late dinner and now people on the street were blowing on paper horns and wearing cone-shaped sparkling hats. Many were drunk and raucous. It was the way I had pictured VJ and VE days when I was still too young to participate at the end of WW II.

We all stood there looking up and at last the silver ball began to slowly descend from the Times Building announcing 12:00 and the beginning of a new year. The noise level grew to a roar. Shredded paper began falling from the high windows above us.

Gilly kissed me. So did some strange fellow standing alongside of us. It was all okay. It was New Year's Eve. And I was in the best place in the world. My life would never again appear so full of hope and promise and naivete. I recalled my favorite line from

The Tempest, which I spoke out loud. When Caliban (the misfit) tries to calm and reassure the visitors to his island world, he speaks the words that also gave me comfort.

> "*Be not afeard,*
> *The isle is full of noises,*
> *Sounds and sweet airs that give delight and hurt not*"

A few days later, peering through the window of the plane, the skyline grew more distant, until it disappeared covered by a layer of clouds. I returned to Miami, to my teaching position, furnished apartment and pristine beaches; away from my family, my roots, and the magic of growing up in a place of hopeful optimism where anything could happen. I never saw Gil again.

Welcome to Los Angeles

I STOOD ON THE CURB watching the cans of Campbell's soup roll into the gutter, grabbing onto what I could with one hand, while stopping my four-year-old from running into the road after the others. The cars whizzed by the corner of Lankershim and Ventura as I frantically scrambled to retrieve the groceries that had ripped through the brown bags in both my arms. No one stopped. No one even slowed down.

Welcome to Los Angeles.

THE ASTHMA OF MY childhood had returned in Miami with its sticky humidity that spawned fungus and mold and left me gasping for air. At twenty-seven years old, I was much too young to live on weekly cortisone injections and keep an oxygen tank in my bedroom for emergencies. I needed to leave this climate.

"Please get me out of here. I need to go somewhere I can breathe," I begged the man who married me knowing I was in love with someone else.

Harold was tall, pleasant-looking, and some said good-looking. I never noticed. From behind his horn-rimmed glasses were pale blue eyes. His hair was curly and dark and his skin white. He sunburned easily and in another twelve years, at the age of forty, he would die from malignant melanoma. Because he was a Jewish attorney, my parents approved of him instantly, which was the kiss of death for me. Anyone they liked had to be all wrong for me. They never knew who I was so how could they know what I needed? Harold never had appealed to me. The most compelling reason for this marriage was that I didn't love him. I could never be hurt or devastated by his actions or words. It was safe to marry someone I could leave.

"I need to get away from these allergies," I argued.

"You're allergic to me," he said. "You'll probably be sick wherever you go."

"Come with us," I pleaded. Even in this marriage of safety, it was still scary to face the world alone again, this time with a small child. Had he been willing to go, the rest of the story might have been different.

"I can't just leave my law practice. How can I leave my mother alone here?" He sealed our fates with that remark. Frances was a young fifty-year-old, fully employed, in good health and so limber she could do the splits.

One year later, Harold acted stunned when he was served with divorce papers. If only he'd said what I needed to hear; if only he had said, "Darling, of course I'll get you out of here. Your health is everything. I love you and I want to take care of you." If only...but he didn't. And it became clear I was on my own, as always.

I saved my weekly pittance of leftover grocery allowance for a year and bought a plane ticket to L.A, taking with me the child whose life I was about to ruin. She never forgave me for taking her away from her father. I carried her onto the plane wrapped in a blanket, since children under four could fly for free.

"If they ask how old you are, say you're three years old."

"Okay, Mommy." She looked up into my face. "I'm three," she giggled, thinking this was a new game. Her brown curls grazed my cheek.

When we were belted into our seats, I looked out of the window. I was not sorry to leave. I never liked Miami. I came to Florida "just for the winter," which turned into seven years. Now I was fleeing again. I saw the palm trees in the distance lining the airfield. I would never return to this place, or to this marriage. I was leaving it all behind: my '53 Chevy parked in the driveway, my new house still not completely furnished, my wedding gifts, and the husband I never loved and the marriage that provided a safe place to go after the man I loved abandoned me. I took the baby and our clothes. Nothing else. I couldn't breathe.

I would never again see the pink and blue rocking horse, Terrie's circus bedroom with the striped red and white awnings, the trampoline in the back yard which we bought to save the king-size mattress on our bed from her leaps of joy. I would never again see the infant layette and all the precious pink organdy baby dresses packed away for the next baby who was not to be. I would never again see my bone china, the silver wedding gifts, the crystal stemware, my beautiful sunken living room with the white brick fireplace, and my new Singer sewing machine that I was learning to use.

I had talked about getting out of Miami's deadly climate for two years. Harold never heard or took me seriously. I desperately needed to be heard and cared about. He ended each conversation with "I can't leave."

He underestimated my determination. On the day I announced I was leaving on my own with the baby, he didn't believe me. But his mother was overjoyed. She had waited to reclaim him from the day we married. She was a pretty little woman with a Russian accent. She always called him, "My son the counselor." And now she had the colossal nerve to say to me, "Dear, if you had let me know you were going to California, I would have made you a going away party." I was stunned. She thought I was going on a vacation? But I knew she was in a celebratory mood, finally getting rid of me. She had been deeply critical of me, something I was accustomed to growing up with disapproving parents. She told her son she was "lonely" and he moved her into the small duplex apartment we had rented shortly after the baby was born.

I was frantic. Every night in our bed after the lights were out, I whispered to him, "You have to get your mother out of here. She can't live with us."

"How can I put my own mother on the street?" he said.

The nights were long. She slept on the living room sofa on the other side of our bedroom wall. She complained every morning. "Dear, the light from the window wakes me up. Can you hang up darker drapes? The sofa has lumps in it." I once jokingly told her she reminded me of the princess and the pea. Coming from Russia, she had never heard that fairytale and I didn't explain it to her.

I never told her she was wrecking my marriage. But late at night when we lay in bed in the dark, I pleaded with Harold. "Please, let's find a place for your mother to live."

He couldn't do it. I had married a mamma's boy.

The only time he was exciting or dynamic was when he gave closing arguments to a jury in a criminal trial. Then he became a young Perry Mason. But the passive man I lived with couldn't tell his mother she was intruding in our lives.

She stayed with us for over a year, entertaining her friends in the art world with weekly exhibitions of her oil paintings. Her framed, splashy, gaudy blobs of color with no particular form stood around the periphery of the living room. My one-year-old sat in her playpen in the same room, breathing the toxic fumes from the paints and oils.

"Dear, please serve some snacks to my friends," she told me. And like a sheep, I obeyed her and entertained "the artists." I took orders from her, never arguing. I was as passive as her son…at least on the surface. But I was saving it all up. Finally she left us for a job in Washington, D.C. She was a seamstress and Wardrobe Mistress for celebrities. A job offer came and I exhaled a sigh of relief. She was out of there, for now.

Terrie was two years old, and I wanted a home. I hunted everywhere and finally found an inexpensive, newly built house in Perrine, Florida, just outside of the Everglades. It was a lovely three-bedroom home on a cul de sac street and I fell in love with it. When I excitedly told Harold I found our dream home, he said,

"How do you think we're going to pay for it?"

I assumed we had a nest egg from all the cash wedding gifts and money from my parents and all my savings that I had trusted him to put into our joint account.

"We'll use the savings," I explained. I had a sinking feeling in my stomach. Had I missed something?

"What do you think we've been living on?" He stared blankly at me as if I was worse than naive; as if I was stupid to not know that.

"I thought you were earning it," I said, confirming my ignorance.

Never again would I trust anyone with my money. This was a man who had a new car every year, wore custom made suits and a law office that he furnished lavishly. The back wall of the waiting room revealed a large aquarium with exotic fish swimming in it. We didn't have a bedspread or kitchen table. He explained that it would help to build a business if he presented a nice office, nice car and nice appearance. I had to ask for every penny I wanted to

marian silverman

spend. Never again would I be put in a dependent position or have to ask for a bedspread. Somehow I managed to squirrel away money from my weekly allotment for household expenses and food, and in less than a year, I presented him with the down payment for one of those tract homes in Perrine. We moved in and took our bed, dresser, Terrie's crib and dresser, her rocking horse and the rocking chair I fed her in when she was an infant. The house never got furnished.

I stayed a year. When his mother completed her contract in Washington, she called him to say that she was on her way back to Florida. I heard him on the phone. It was happening again. She was coming to live with us. Before he had hung up the receiver, I pulled my suitcase down from the top of the closet and threw it on the bed. He looked stunned. And coward that he was, told her, "No, you can't come...well...because Marian doesn't want it."

So much for marrying a man who could stand up to his mother. I didn't leave that day, but it was coming soon. I could not breathe in Florida. He sealed our fates by not caring enough about me to take me out of there.

And then I was given one of those great moments in life, where you get to say whatever you want because there is nothing more to lose. On the day I was leaving Florida with my baby and all of our clothing and an airline ticket to Los Angeles, his mother came to the house to say goodbye. She was visibly cheerful at my departure. And I got to say the words that had been playing in my head for a few years.

"Mom," (Why had I agreed to call her that?) "I realize you want him more than I do. I'm going to give him back to you." My finest moment. She was speechless.

They say when "snow bunnies" leave New York, they go to either Florida or California. Florida felt like the end of the world. From Miami there was nowhere to go except to the Keys or

Havana. And then after Castro liberated Cuba, the nights of hopping a plane and dancing in the open-air Copacabana nightclubs were over, and Cuba was closed to us forever. Easy, legal and safe abortions for desperate young girls were no longer available for the price of a 30-minute plane ride and $150.

Lyn met us at the airport. She took one look at me holding my toddler in my arms with bags slung over both shoulders and said in her typical cut-to-the-chase fashion, "Do you know what you're doing?"

The answer was easy. I said, "No."

She blithely accepted that and loaded us into her old VW camper bus and took us home with her. We stayed there for a week. Her husband was agreeable and really liked Terrie.

"If I thought they'd all turn out like this one, I'd consider having one," he said. Two years later they did.

Lyn took several sick days from teaching and drove us around to look for an apartment in North Hollywood where she lived, while Terrie napped in the back of the VW. Always the same story, as I stood at front doors of apartment buildings, reading the words "no children" above the mailboxes. Each time I climbed back into the bus, Terrie heard me repeat the line, "no children," and at the end of the day she would innocently ask me if I'd found any children for her to play with.

I finally found a depressing little apartment that looked like a cold water walk-up flat. The gaudy banners streaming over the front of the building announced children welcome and in case you missed that, you could hear the din of noisy children running around and screaming as you approached. I wanted to run. Each time a door had slammed with "Sorry, no children," Terrie understood it to mean that there were no children there for her, and not that she was the unwanted one. This broke my heart, but it was less painful than the alternative so I never told her otherwise.

Every night she would ask, "Mommy, did you find any children today?"

"Yes," I said finally, "I did."

The apartment was awful, but I had to take it. Since I had no car, in order to get supplies and groceries, we walked several blocks to the nearest market, making a few trips, and I'd given her the light paper goods to carry. We were almost home when the weight of the cans of soup broke the paper bags in both of my arms. The cars flew by. I thought, what kind of place is this that people would not stop to help a woman and child running after groceries in the street? Surely they saw us. Even New Yorkers were not this anonymous.

It was looking bad for L.A. as a refuge. Terrie got sick with flu; I got sick with bronchial asthma again. I was discouraged. This was why I had left Florida. We lasted through six weeks of paid rent. Then I couldn't take it anymore, bought a one-way bus ticket to Arizona, and shipped a trunk with all our clothes to general delivery in Phoenix. I called a motel listed in my Auto Club book that rented by the week and had a pool, and got on a bus at ten o'clock at night. We arrived about six in the morning. A portly, red-faced man from the motel met us at the bus terminal. As he carried my luggage to his van, I could see him breathing heavily. He was having an asthma attack. My luggage must have been too heavy for him. I asked him if he was in the desert for his asthma. He wheezed yes. I knew I was in trouble. So much for geography.

I STAYED LONG ENOUGH to rent an apartment in Scottsdale, get a teaching position, buy a car, make some friends, obtain a master's from ASU, and establish residency to get a divorce. I started breathing again. I discovered I could take care of myself.

Harold called when he was served with divorce papers. "Why

are you putting me at arm's distance?" His voice was more than surprised. It was indignant.

I exploded. "Arm's distance? We haven't seen each other for a year. You never came to see Terrie. She cried for you every night and watched by the window for your car. What do you mean, arm's distance?"

He had no answer except the pathetic line that said it all. "I've broken it off with my mother." To stupidly admit that there was anything to break off, that in fact he had been so involved with her that it had to be "broken off" assured me I had made the right decision. It was over.

He believed I would come back to Florida and left my old Chevy standing in the carport for over a year.

I reminded him that he had refused to come with us when I was scared, that he had said I would be sick wherever I went and that I was just allergic to him. I reminded him that on Mother's Day he went to visit his mother and never gave me so much as a gift or card, explaining that after all I wasn't his mother. And now that I was filing for divorce, he sent me a pearl on a chain for Mother's Day, as if to compensate for the three years he did nothing.

"Too little, too late," I had written him as a thank you note. I loved that I got to say that. It was perfect. I didn't need him. I had done it all by myself, as always.

I stayed in Arizona long enough to be sure I hated the desert. Waking up to the view of cacti from my window, and dry dull mountains instead of the ocean was deadly.

Our days in the desert were numbered. By the fourth year, I interviewed for a teaching position in San Diego, got it and drove myself and my seven-and-a-half-year-old daughter back to California. I announced to my friends that I was going to San Diego to start a new life, get married, and be happy.

Well, the first two happened. But the journey was far from over. Eventually I would land back in L.A. Eventually I would see L.A. through different eyes, eventually it would be home. But that's another story.

Good Luck, Paul, I Hope You Catch the Red Shadow

SHIMMERING IN THE SUN'S reflection, the aircraft's silver wings dipped dramatically over the gray skyline of my gray city. Waves of nausea washed over me as we approached the runway to La Guardia field. The flight from Phoenix was rough and bumpy, with sudden drops of altitude that left me sick. Coming home to visit my parents for the first time since my divorce, with my five-year-old child, I was prepared to face their disapproval once again. Another failure!

"Are we there yet, Mommy?"

"Yes, sweet girl. This is New York, where Mommy grew up."

"I want to see Nanny and Poppa."

"We'll see them soon, baby, soon." Too soon, I thought.

"And Uncle Robert too?"

"Yes...I hope so."

My dear brother, will you be there for me? When did I first lose you?

I REMEMBER SITTING AT the breakfast table across from him when I was ten. "I'm not looking at you," I said. Together we lined up the cereal box, milk container, juice jar and anything else we could use as barriers so we couldn't see each other. My mother didn't seem to mind, so we thought that this was common sibling behavior. But I also remember that he was my hero.

"My brother'll get you," I warned the boys that chased me home from school, pelting me with snowballs. "I'm telling my brother on you." Racing up the hallway stairs, I yelled, "Rob—Robert!" My woolen snowsuit was covered with evidence of the attack, small white powdered explosions.

"What happened?" He jumped up, ready for action. And then began the infamous lists he wrote, while I called out the names of those responsible: "Eddie—Jackie—Howie—um—those sixth-grade boys. I don't know the other ones. They just don't like me." It was like putting out contracts. I never knew if he beat them up, but those same boys never bothered me again. For only he was allowed to batter me and only when I deserved it.

He was also assigned to take me to school in the morning. I would cling tightly to his hand, terrified I'd get lost in the mammoth school yard of Public School 225 in Brooklyn, where thousands of small persons waited like prisoners behind the numbered posts that designated their class and room assignment.

"My sister is so dumb," he would complain to his buddies, "she doesn't even know what line to get on." And echoes of that for years afterward. My identity was set.

I'M CONVINCED THAT IN most families, there is a good child and a bad child. I think these role assignments serve to keep the family together. Everyone knows their parts. Strengths and weaknesses are well defined. My brother and I were given our roles for life, like a curse. There was no escape. As the problem child, the dumb kid, often the sick one, I made both of my parents feel strong, capable and smart. I suspect I was there to help them with their own self-doubts and fears. They had a focus; helping me.

My brother stayed in their good graces by carrying out their orders. Although I had long ago accepted the role of the damaged and defective child, until I grew up I never realized the price my brother paid for his privileged title of the good kid. I wondered how long we would continue to accept our family's definition of who we were!

"Welcome to New York," the flight attendant announced. "We thank you for flying with us and wish you a pleasant stay."

I shivered and unlocked our seat belts. Looking out the window, I saw them clearly, standing hopefully at the top level of the observation deck, arms waving, coats blowing open. My mother wore that peculiar brown felt hat with the fringes hanging down the side of her face like droppings from a bird's nest. My dad had on his Dick Tracy fedora with the crease down the middle. Yes, there they were, my inheritance.

"Let's put your sweater and coat on, *zeis kindt*." Suddenly I became my Jewish mother. I swore I'd never be her. And yet those words came out of my mouth. I was home.

All I really wanted was to be acceptable, god forbid, even liked, but this was not in our family script. My brother, the good child, was part of the design to keep me feeling inadequate. "Take care of your sister," they told him. "She needs help."

I realize now that his survival depended on my weakness. He had taken on the attributes of the prison guards. How much easier to be the bad child. I played my part. I had to be dumb, needy, and afraid.

The two-story brick house with the storm windows looked much as it had twenty years ago, a grim reminder of early imprisonment. Once inside, the rooms offered the same clutter of curios on glass shelves, ceramic figurines, miniature collections of glass animals and the china tea set enshrined forever on what my mother referred to as "the fifty-dollar coffee table," something she purchased during the Depression. Rob and I smiled at each other every time we heard, "Take your feet off the fifty-dollar coffee table." When no one was home, I'd sit with my feet up on top of it.

There were no blank spaces; even the walls were covered with family photographs. I had difficulty breathing in this house, and remembered the onset of childhood asthma. In the center of the living room, framed in ornate antique gold, hung a huge wedding portrait facing a wall of mirrors, so that the room was filled with my wedding.

"Oh god!" I said. "Mother, I'm divorced. You can take that thing down now."

"Why?" She shrugged. "It's a good picture of you."

And off she trotted to the kitchen, her favorite retreat. During the war, when she worked, she would rush in the door, head straight for the kitchen, remove her dress and hurriedly tie on her apron. There she stood hovering near the kitchen stove wearing her apron over a slip, with a hat still on her head.

I had to remind myself that this was the same harmless-looking woman who had interfered in my brother's life. She just found out he was dating my high school friend who—god help us—was not Jewish.

"I forbid you to see her anymore," she pronounced, her arms crossed in front of her.

I was in the next room, listening. That stung. She was my friend. She had been to our house often and I had no idea that she was good enough for me, but not for my brother. I was insulted.

"I don't tell you who to be friends with!" Rob yelled back at her. Surprised to hear him defending himself, I stood behind the kitchen door, silently cheering him on. His words surpassed my wildest hopes. "What makes you think I like your friends?"

Tell her, I thought. My mother and I had always yelled at each other, but I didn't expect this from the two of them.

He went on. "Do you think I like Rose Goldstein, that annoying gossip you play mah jong with? Or Shirley Adler with that high-pitched voice and phony mannerism? Don't ever tell me who to have in my life."

It was the only time I ever heard him stand up to her. He protested loudly, and for one wild and brave moment, he was my hero again. He was free, I thought. But he had learned early and well what his survival was to be in that house, and he never went out with my friend again. Eventually he married someone more like his mother. He had learned he must cooperate with the enemy, like Jews trying to survive Auschwitz by adopting the basic attitudes of their jailers.

But I also carried a memento of his imprisonment in my school graduation album. On a shiny blue page he wrote, "Always be good to your parents, they'll only be happy when you are." Of all the challenges and wondrous excitement that life might hold for me, of all the life affirming things that he could have said, this was all he could think to say to me. My poor brother, the good son. I shuddered even then to realize he had sold out.

The next day my brother arrived. He lived in Long Island, and saw my parents often, so presumably he came to see me. My mother hovered over us constantly. She never left us alone together. Rob and I had not seen each other in a few years and apparently were not to be allowed the visit I longed for. My mother seemed to always be in the room, until one brief and wonderful moment that I will remember forever. Alone in my parents' bedroom, we looked into each other's eyes, knowing that at any instant, we would be interrupted and it would be over. I looked at his great face, a face that women have always been attracted to. At thirty-five, his hairline had already begun to recede so that he would become his bald father. Rob had a reassuring smile that opened into a broad grin. But it was his eyes that I always watched closely; sad brown eyes that held back pain, with tears just behind the lids. I wondered what we could possibly say to each other now that would make a difference. There was so much to remember. The music and themes of our childhood kept playing in my head.

OUR FIRST RECORD WAS played on an old wind-up Victrola that lived its days in the basement of our house in Brooklyn. It was becoming obsolete, already an antique in the late forties. We had only 78 rpm records. We pooled our resources and bought a turntable phonograph and our first album, Sigmund Romberg's *The Desert Song* with the Broadway cast of Dennis Morgan and Kitty Carlisle Hart at the unheard-of speed of 33 1/3 rpm. I would sing the entire score while my father walked through the house closing windows. The lyrics thrilled me.

> *Blue Heaven and you and I*
> *And sand kissing a moonlit sky*
> *The desert breeze whispering a lullaby*
> *Only stars about you*
> *To see I love you*

The operetta tells of an ordinary, shy and nondescript character named Paul who falls in love with Margo, a beautiful heroine. Paul is actually the masked outlaw of the desert, "The Red Shadow," whom Margo secretly adores. This dual character ends up rescuing her, saving the desert from evil forces and riding off into the sunset with the girl in his arms. But it was the lead-in dialogue to that title song that became most memorable to me.

For when Paul, on the side of the law, sets out to capture the outlaw, he bids his love farewell, promising to return the desert to its natural destiny. As he rides away, Margo calls out in her mezzo soprano voice, the silly words:

"Good luck, Paul, I hope you catch the Red Shadow." It was the only spoken line in the operetta. Inevitably this became my parting shot to my brother each time he left me in the house with *them*. He usually laughed, waved and left anyway. He was always leaving.

Rob moved on from the good son who always did what he was told to the good husband who worked two jobs, then came home and vacuumed the house. He was as devoted to his family as he had been to his parents, never showing his feelings except for eyes about to cry. In contrast to this, my life continued to be a soap-opera of one disaster after another, turbulent unhappy relationships, and now the worst crime my mother had to whisper behind her cupped hand: "divorced."

I was considered rebellious, since I tried to find my own way. My brother was considered devoted since he opted for controlled safety and never left home at all. So now, here we were facing each other with an unspoken history of pain and tears and memories, touching and troubled. I felt doubtful we could ever bridge the gaps. We stood there reaching for some sort of connection, some meaning to all of it.

"Well, kid, did you find out what line to get on?"

I was still for a moment, absorbing that question.

I was alone again, still scared, a lost child wanting my brother to take my hand and walk me to a safe spot.

"No," I answered, watching his eyes.

Swollen tears welled up from somewhere behind old hurt. And although I didn't know it then, this was all there was to be for us; we would never be close again in the way we were as children. We had our own journeys to take, and they would lead us in different directions, away from each other.

I must have sensed an ending as I packed to leave New York and return home to Arizona the following day. I didn't know how long he had been standing in the doorway watching me. I couldn't trust myself to look at him. My father loaded the suitcases into the car with his usual warmth.

"It's late...hurry up...let's go...you're gonna' miss your flight."

I left the house carrying the child who was too young to understand any of this—marriage, divorce, loneliness, brothers—and got into the back of my father's old green Chevy.

It was starting to snow as we pulled away from the house I had grown up in. I looked up to see that framed in the window was my brother's sad face. Frantically I tried to roll down the tight car window. It was stuck.

The car pulled away from the curb. I managed to force it open, leaned out as far as I could, and called out at the top of my voice, and for all I was ever worth.

Good luck, Paul, I hope you catch the Red Shadow.

If Your Father Doesn't Love You...

I DIDN'T WANT TO write about my father. He wounded me with a sharp edged sword called criticism that severed my heart and raped my ego. I hated him because I thought he didn't love me. I didn't want to write about him because I thought the pain would kill me, the way looking into a solar eclipse without sunglasses would blind me. Yet I must look and I must write or I will never be free to love myself.

MY FATHER NEVER LIKED me. He said everything I did was wrong. He would show me that he could do it better. I tried to make him like me. I tried to do everything right. I failed.

When I was eight years old, playing with a puzzle, I noticed him watching me from across the room as I slowly fit the pieces together. He got up, walked over, and took a piece out of my hand, saying, "Here, that's not right. Let me show you how to do it." He put the entire puzzle together for me. I lost interest in puzzles immediately. And so it went with anything I tried. It was always wrong. I was always wrong. I was incompetent. I was not a good girl.

My father was competent at everything he did, from the plumbing to the painting of the house, to the electrical appliances he fixed by himself. He was patient and took his time until he got it done. When any of my toys broke, I picked up the shattered pieces in my hands and brought them to him, expecting him to put them together. He could do anything.

I thought he was superman. I could never measure up, and he always reminded me of that fact. "You didn't do that right," was the usual commentary. I don't remember his ever hugging me, showing me any affection, or even saying, "Good job."

If your father doesn't love you, who will? If you're a girl and your father doesn't love you, what man will?

When my brother was sent to Hebrew School, I pleaded to go too. It was just for boys becoming men, my father explained. "Besides," he said, "Hebrew is much too difficult for you, you'll never learn it."

I believed him. It was too difficult for me. I wasn't smart enough.

Sports were ruled out as well. "You'll freeze to death in the snow if you go skiing. You'll fall and won't be able to get up."

There was an ice rink in downtown Brooklyn where all the high school kids went to skate. I went along once and sat in the stands watching the cute teen age girls in short skirts go round the rink in their white shoe skates. I could never do that, I thought. I just looked at them and how pretty they were, and listened to the organ music.

I asked my father if I could have ice skates for Chanukah. Maybe I could learn. "Oh, you'll fall down" he said. "It's hard to stand on a single blade." Yet I had seen girls and boys my same age of thirteen standing and even spinning around on them. I wanted to try.

Opening the gift box on the first night of Chanukah, I gasped. Inside the box were skates. Then I looked closer and saw the shoes had double blades. They were learner skates—for little kids. I dropped the box on the floor and ran into my room, slammed the door and threw myself on my bed, crying. I will never be anything, I thought. I will never do anything well. I am defective. There is something wrong with me.

There was a saying around my house. If something was very easy, or required little ability, my father would say, "That's so easy, even Marian could do it." I heard that a lot. It became the benchmark for my incompetence. It became my definition of myself.

"The early bird catches the worm," he would call out as he poked his head into my room on a Saturday morning at eight a.m. "Don't waste your day in bed, don't be lazy." He had no idea of the sleep needs of an adolescent. Sleeping in was wrong. No wonder I still suffer from insomnia and feel guilty if I sleep or relax.

Yet, I have an early memory of sitting in my stroller being walked by my father along Sheepshead Bay. I could not have been more than one or two, maybe three years of age. Some say memory doesn't record that early. But what is remarkable isn't how young I was to remember this, but that my father actually took me for walks at all. This is the father I thought never liked me. Yet there he was, pushing me alongside the Bay area where I could see the houseboats rocking from side to side, smell the salty water and listen to the raucous seagulls. I knew that he was my daddy and that he was proud of me.

WHEN DID HE STOP loving me? What did I do wrong?

While visiting an elderly aunt (my father's sister) in Florida, a revelation was offered to me. My Aunt Stella lived in a nursing care facility. I had come to visit her with my father and her daughter, my cousin Tessa. An attendant wheeled her out to the pool area to visit with us. She sat bent over in the hospital chair, her body folded in half. Years of suffering with asthma gave her chest a caved in look. She smiled broadly when she saw me.

"Oh, Marian, my favorite niece," she said. I gave her a hug and she hugged me back. Her hair was pure white, and her face was wrinkled and weatherworn from years of living in Florida, always out in the sun, and like everyone else in Florida, working twelve months a year to keep a tan going. But she still looked like my Aunt Stella. I always liked her—probably because she liked me. Whenever I came to visit, she made a fuss over me, and directed her stories to me. My aunt did love to talk and tell stories.

My mother had just died, and my Aunt began reminiscing about when I was born, and when I was a baby, and how cute, and pretty, and smart I was. My father said nothing. She looked directly at him when she said it. "Your father was so crazy about you."

I held my breath. He was? How did I miss that?

She went on. "Yes, he couldn't get enough of you, just never took his eyes off you, at least in the beginning. Then they got to him, and he changed."

At this point my cousin interrupted. "Mom, would you like a lemonade? Would anyone like a lemonade? They can bring them out to us."

"No, dear," said my aunt. "Let me tell Marian what happened to her."

There was no stopping her. I felt a pain growing in my stomach. My head felt light and dizzy. Everyone knew something I didn't know, and now it was going to be told, like it or not. My father sat there silently.

"Well," she continued on, oblivious to everyone's discomfort. "I remember when Robert started holding his breath." No one spoke. But she didn't seem to care. I guess when you're in your nineties you get to say whatever you want.

"He held his breath whenever he didn't get what he wanted, and your father gave him anything he wanted. Herman couldn't stand it when Robert started to turn blue from holding his breath. He said, 'I never want to see him like that. Give him whatever he wants.' Well, your father spoiled him, so everyone said."

Now my father sat up in his chair. "Stel," he tried to cut her off.

"No Herman, let me talk." As if anyone could stop her now. "After you were born, your mother warned him—don't you spoil this one. That's what she said. That's what everyone told him. But not me. I thought it was wrong. And what happened was wrong."

My father began to squirm in his chair. Then, without looking at me, with eyes cast down, he said, "Well, they were all on my back about how I spoiled Robert, how it was my fault he held his breath. So I decided not to have anything to do with *this* one, this new baby," he said, still looking down at the ground. "Then they couldn't blame me. In the beginning, I took you out for walks. Then I was warned again. So I just started staying away from spoiling or doing anything wrong." He looked directly at me. "I left it to your mother."

After that, I was too numb to remember anything else in the conversation. In fact, I remember nothing more about that day. My mother did this? I had always blamed him—no, I always blamed myself. There had to be something wrong with *me*. If your father doesn't love you, who will?

After the numbness, there was no great relief, no lifting of sorrow, no reconciliation. There is a time when a child needs a father. If it doesn't happen then, it's too late. And it doesn't matter why, it only matters that you didn't feel love. There is no explanation that will suffice.

No matter how hard I tried to be what my father wanted, I never could win his love. I tried to please him. I tried to be perfect. I was never good enough. My father, a postal worker, uneducated, having to drop out of elementary school in the sixth grade in order to help his family working in their grocery store, later resented his female child for going to college.

I was studying psychology, and he found a book with a chapter on sexual deviants.

"For this I'm sending you to college? Get married. Whatta ya need this for?"

He was not sending me to college. I actually was attending a city college with no tuition or expenses, and lived at home, working for my personal expenses. But, there was no pleasing him.

If you're a girl, and your father doesn't love you, what man will?

I tried to have the perfect child. Maybe I could get that right and be a perfect mother. I had a perfect child. She was born perfect. But instead I made her neurotic. My daughter grew up hating me for taking her away from her father and for dragging her all over the country. She chewed up her fingernails. She was not able to please me, either. I did to her what my father had done to me. I failed relationships, marriage, motherhood.

The night my mother died, I chose not to return to Florida for the funeral. I had no more goodbyes to say. This decision stunned my brother. In the morning when I spoke with my father, his response caused me to nearly drop the phone. Never in my life had he ever given me a positive word of concern, or caring. I didn't go to the funeral. But this was a new father, one I didn't recognize.

After that, I called him without the usual dread. I would hang up the phone after a long distance call and notice that I wasn't shaking. He would ask me how I was. *How I was?* He began asking me how my dog was, although he never remembered her name. It didn't matter; I would remind him about Holly. We had something to talk about besides the weather and the price of gasoline in California, or my failures.

I thought perhaps he just missed my mother and had decided to be nicer to me. But after the day with my aunt, I realized that the censor had been removed and he was free to express his feelings toward me, feelings that he always had and submerged in order to placate my mother.

I talked it over with my therapist. "What happened?" I asked him. "Why now?"

My therapist explained that the intense love and attraction of fathers toward their daughters is threatening to insecure mothers, and that they covertly pull them from that relationship in any way they can.

He smiled and said, "Well, you have your father back now."

I said, "No, I needed a father all my life, but not now. It's too late."

My father lived until his one hundredth birthday. He had announced that he would make it to that occasion. And as always, he was right. I had told him I wasn't angry anymore. But I never told him I loved him. The damage was done.

White Rose

I LOST HIM SLOWLY, gradually, in agony and grief. My worst fear was that he would leave me. He told me in a thousand ways that he would never stay with me. I didn't believe him.

THERE IS A MOMENT FROZEN in time that I remember. It was one of those non-dramatic, uneventful scenes that would change the course of my life. The setting is MacArthur Beach Park in Miami. It is 1957.

I spend my weekends lying in the sun, tanning. Looking good is of the utmost importance. No worries about skin cancer. I quote, "Live fast, die young and make a good-looking corpse." I can't imagine being forty or fifty, or having sun-damaged skin. It is all about now. It is all about being attractive.

I lie on my stomach with sun-streaked blonde hair falling below thin shoulders, wearing a one-piece aqua-colored swimsuit. Long tanned legs stretch out far beyond the beach towel. A stack of second grade writing papers are spread out in front of me. I red-pencil the shaky beginning efforts at printing of my seven-year-old students.

Some twenty feet away, a young man watches, staring at me as he lies sprawled in the sand, one hand propped under his head. I feel his gaze, but keep my eyes down so as not to make eye contact. I am used to being watched on the beach.

He is walking toward me. I glance at him briefly and notice that he is a little overweight, has a roll of fat around his waist, smooth skin and round sloping shoulders. His hair is in a crewcut that doesn't suit him. I am unimpressed.

He says, "Hi."

I nod politely, return my focus to the papers and ignore him.

He stands there, awkwardly waiting. "What are you working on?" he asks.

"My kids' papers," I say.

He watches me, as if unable to pull himself away, or too dumb to take the hint.

What a jerk, I think.

Finally he walks off. Later, he repeats the same scenario, asks another inane question, stands around, and finally slumps away to leave me to my solitude.

I watch him leave and feel relieved of his intense stare.

This boring scene persists for the next few Sundays, with his approach and my disinterest. It is always the same. He tells me he is a law student at the University of Miami and is twenty-seven years old. His name is David.

There would be no way to tell that I would ultimately become obsessed with this man for the next twenty years; no way to predict that he would be the love of my life, the one that got away, the only one I could never have, and that I would be suicidal one year from now when he left me. This man who appeared obsessive in his interest would leave me five times. I could never get him to stay. I would never get over him. I would never forget him. Watching this scene, there would be no way to tell any of this, no way to tell at all.

One Sunday, he changes the routine and follows me as I leave the beach and head toward my car.

"Would you like to go get a beer later?" he asks as I slide into my front seat.

I shrug and hear myself say, "All right." What am I thinking? Maybe this might finally get rid of him? "Pick me up at seven," I say as I scribble my address on a scrap of paper. At home, standing in the shower rinsing the sand from my long hair, I regret making the date. Why am I going out with this guy? I don't like him. He's annoying. But it is too late. He is already on his way over.

It's a warm night and I slip into a yellow sleeveless cotton dress and sandals, my bare legs covered with baby oil to give their golden tan a shine. I stopped wearing hose after leaving New York. Men tell me I have great legs. And this is Miami, the land of sunshine and sun tans. I am told I look like the golden girl on the billboard for Coppertone sunscreen.

David arrives at seven promptly. He pauses behind the screen door holding a freshly lit cigarette in his hand. He just lit up; I can still smell the match. I think he must be insecure to need the cigarette to hold onto like a prop before he can muster the courage to ring the doorbell. The realization that he's nervous goes through my mind. This evening is really important to him. It is of little significance to me.

We walk to his car, a green Ford convertible with the top down. He drives to a small bar on the beach. He does not offer me anything to eat, just orders two beers. He's a third-year law student and apparently doesn't have the money to take me to dinner. Good! A shorter evening and I can get away sooner. Then hopefully he'll leave me alone.

It turns out differently than I expect. We sit on wooden benches facing each other, grasping heavy glass beer mugs by the thick handles. He never takes his eyes off me. He spends two hours asking questions about my life. "Where did you grow up? What is your family like? Do you have siblings? What do you like to do? What did you study in school? Who are your friends? Who is your favorite composer? Do you love Sinatra?"

I answer all his questions. Oh my, yes, I do love Sinatra. The evening is all about me. He listens, hanging on every word. His eyes never leave my face. He is more interested in me than anyone has ever been. My family never seemed to hear me or know much about what I thought, or what I liked. For the first time somebody is listening with great interest to what I have to say. I tell him "my story." And slowly I begin to have a good time listening to myself talk. And watching his interest grow.

I talk about my brother, about studying psychology, loving romantic poets, loving the theatre and growing up in New York, my city. And he listens. He becomes interesting simply because he is interested in me.

When he takes me home, he does not make a pass at me like most of my dates. He says goodnight without a kiss or touch. He walks me to my door, his eyes shining with interest and longing. I open the screen door of my small furnished apartment and go inside, kick off my shoes and curl up on the sofa. What a surprise. I actually had a good time. Yes, I will go out with him again when he calls me, probably tomorrow.

But he doesn't call. The days roll by and the phone doesn't ring. I am puzzled and confused about this man.

"God, did I read this wrong," I say to one of my friends at school. "I was sure he'd call right away. He seemed so taken with me." I shrug it off. It's okay to never see him again, just unusual that I made a mistake in assessing his interest which appeared so strong. I think of him several times in the next week. I wonder why he didn't call me. I was sure he would. I am not invested, just surprised that he hasn't called when it was he who had pursued me so relentlessly, and he who had hung on my every word and look.

"I was so sure he was interested in me," I say to my friend on the second week without a phone call.

My underlying lack of confidence surfaces, and I wonder if I have done something wrong. Maybe I talked too much about myself. He certainly has my interest now. By the third week, with no phone call, I decide to forget about him.

One evening as I sit cross legged on the sofa, again correcting my kids' papers, I hear a tapping on the screen door and a vaguely familiar voice.

"Hi, teacher." I look up and see David through the screen, standing like a school boy in white shorts and a tee shirt, holding a bouquet of red roses. I open the door and smile at this amazing sight.

"Hello," I say. I am charmed by the flowers, and relieved that he has come back. He answers the unspoken question.

"I wanted to see you again." I feel my heart race. He doesn't look so bad. I have to ask. "Where'd you go, what happened to you?" The answer he gives will stay with me for many years. It will explain the unexplainable long after I fall in love with him, and long after he leaves me.

He looks at me with the sad eyes that would become his trademark. He says the simple words that ring with authenticity, but foreshadow tragedy.

"I liked you too much."

I feel an instant cold chill go through my body. Although it sounds like a compliment, there is something wrong with this answer. People who really like each other don't stay away. I ignore the discomfort in the pit of my stomach. I accept this answer because I feel I've won the lottery. I don't want to recognize the magnitude of his fear. And I don't listen to my instincts, the clear warning signal, the red flag waving in front of my face.

I never imagined anyone could be afraid to like me. Here is a man who runs from feelings so strong they frighten him. But he comes back. He can't stay away. I must be magnetic. I must be lovable. He is unable to be without me. This is compelling. No one has ever liked me "too much." I am hooked.

MY APARTMENT IN MIAMI was part of a duplex on S.W. Eighth Street just outside of Coral Gables, the more affluent neighborhood. As a first-year teacher with no prior training, I knew nothing. I made it up as I went along, yet it turned out to be my most creative year in the classroom. On a provisional teaching credential, I needed six credits a year to maintain it. I relied on pure instinct, a ream of lined writing paper, Number 2 yellow pencils, boxes of Crayola crayons and one set of second grade readers stacked on the floor. That year we put on plays, made crepe paper costumes, danced around the room, read poetry, took long nature walks, and painted freely and wildly on newsprint in rhythm to Ravel's Bolero booming on my portable turntable phonograph. The small hands pounded on their desks, and their feet stomped the floor. This primal display of passion reminded me that I was alive and in love.

Every child learned to read. The principal didn't bother the teachers about curriculum. Unless your class was noisy in the hallways where she was listening, she didn't care what we did behind closed doors.

It was the late 50's. Roe v Wade decision required all public schools be integrated. Central Elementary, in the heart of Miami, was chosen to be among the first of the targeted schools in the country. This was not a problem for me. I was a New York girl, a graduate of Brooklyn College, a liberal school with a multi-ethnic population. When I first arrived in Miami (they called it "Miama") I thought it bizarre when I saw signs reading "Colored" under the water fountains and on restroom doors. I thought it meant that colored water would come out. But I was in the South, no question.

Mrs. White, the principal, was something straight out of Tennessee Williams, even to the point of telling me that when she was a girl, she had many gentleman suitors. Determined to fight the new law, she rebelliously held daily assemblies and stood on the auditorium stage ranting that she'd go down with the school rather than mix with "darkies." I had to keep from laughing out loud each morning when she had us stand and sing *Dixie* while the Confederate flag hung next to the American flag above the stage. We were forced to listen to her protests of "the unfair Federal law." I thought I had gone back to another era. Fear of change was the motivation. But change was coming. Eventually the school became integrated, but by then I was gone.

At the end of each teaching day, I rushed home from school because Dave would be coming over. I thought I had it all: a career that fulfilled me, a man I loved, everything I wanted. It was perfect. When he began to leave a pair of brown shoes in the closet, his beach sandals, an extra shirt, and underwear, I felt he was moving in. But he never gave up the apartment he rented, though he was seldom there and I never saw it. Even then I wondered if it was an escape route in case he needed to flee.

Yet every night I waited for him in my small twin bed, wearing skimpy baby doll pajamas while he sat at the kitchen table studying his law books and drinking beer. I waited for him, for the passion between us, the trembling when we touched. I stayed awake until he came to me. He would tie the twin beds together with ropes so we could sleep touching each other. I could not fall asleep until some part of his body was touching mine, a leg, an arm, a foot. When he wasn't there, I didn't sleep.

He left love notes all over the house that were numbered, and I had to find them like a treasure hunt. He spent the year saying, "I love you." Once he said, "You're going to make some man a wonderful wife. I wish things were different."

I asked, "What things?"

He said, "I can't afford to get married now."

I believed him. I knew we would always be together because we were in love.

But at the end of the spring semester, he packed up his things and left to go to Bethesda Law School in Washington, D.C. for the summer session. He left without asking me to go with him. He kissed me goodbye and asked if I would write.

I said, "No." I didn't want to write letters. I wanted to be with him. He drove away as I looked out of the window. I didn't let him see me cry. I thought, "Be strong, don't be a baby."

The words screamed in my head, "Don't leave me, take me with you." It was the same feeling I had lying on my mother's kitchen floor screaming, "Don't send me away, I'll be good." I knew terror. I knew abandonment.

The next day I wrecked my car in a head-on collision. I was on the six o'clock news, as a miracle, with two other survivors. There were photos of both cars wrapped around a Banyan tree, its many trunks and root systems entwining and trapping us in our vehicles. I wasn't hurt physically, just a few scratches. Without a car, I had to move from the apartment to a rental closer to work. I left the apartment we had shared that had the smell of him in the linens, and his leftover razor blades in the bathroom along with a sweatshirt and a pair of socks he left in the hamper.

I told myself he'd come back for me.

But I couldn't bear the summer without him and decided to

go home to New York, stay with my parents and get the six required credits for my teaching credential at my Alma Mater, Brooklyn College. My mother noticed I had little to say and I think she heard me crying at night, because she commented that I seemed sad. We never talked about my life. It was just a comment.

One month later, at ten o'clock at night, Dave appeared out of nowhere. There was a knock at our kitchen door. My parents, all ready for bed, cautiously opened the door. No one visited at that hour. There he stood, asking for me. How he found my address in Brooklyn I never knew. I came out of my bedroom dressed in a bathrobe and shyly introduced him to my family. They were in shock. My brother, who was married and living in the downstairs apartment, came upstairs to see who was visiting this late at night. Dave lifted me up and whirled me around the room with my stunned parents standing there aghast. Rob gawked.

Later he said, "This guy must be crazy or in love."

I said, "Both."

We were left alone in the living room after everyone went to bed. He had come to take me back to Washington, D.C. with him. Foolish girl that I was, I decided I had suffered too much and never wanted to be left again. I wanted assurances. I thought that was the moment to make my needs known, to make my ultimatum, to tell him I couldn't play house anymore, and that he would need to marry me if he wanted to take me with him. I thought it would prevent him from leaving me, abandoning me, hurting me again; I thought committed would save me from disaster. I also knew my family would never let me go with him.

But he said once again that he simply couldn't get married yet, and he left me there, crying. His eyes welled up with tears as they always did when he was leaving me. I wondered for many years to come what might have been different if I had packed a bag, thrown caution to the winds and gone with him.

By morning I realized I had lost him through this ploy that didn't work. I began to devise a scheme to correct my error. I planned to fly to Washington, D.C., find him, tell him I would be with him anyway I could because I couldn't live without him. This was the truth. I planned this for weeks while finishing Ed classes in summer school at the College. Then I bought a one-way plane ticket, sent a telegram to the P.O. box number I had for him, giving him my flight information. I dressed to kill—all new underwear, high-heeled white pumps, tightly-fitted seersucker suit—and boarded a plane. I was going because I had to be with him.

I was seated in first class for some reason, and there a great-looking guy offered to buy me a drink. But I refused, wanting to be clear when I arrived. No one else interested me.

The plane landed. I was shaking with excitement.

He wasn't there.

In disbelief, I walked around Dulles Airport for three hours, until the personnel began to look at me suspiciously. I didn't cry. I couldn't accept that he didn't come, that he didn't want me. I had blown it by asking to be his wife. I thought he loved me. I never imagined that he never got the telegram, and he'd just met someone he would ultimately marry; this man who couldn't marry me.

Finally I flew back to Miami, and there I hung around the airport, afraid to go home to an empty apartment. I stood in a hot phone booth calling friends who were not at home. Someone please come and get me, or help me. I was too afraid to go home; too afraid I would die of loneliness and grief and rejection. No one answered my calls for help. I took a taxi to my apartment. And then I died. Only I didn't, of course.

School re-opened and I returned to teaching. Hilda, a shiny-faced black cleaning woman at our school, said if the man who had broken my heart ever showed up, she would chase him out of the building with her broom. She was my protector. I should have listened to her.

On a late afternoon in autumn, I walked toward the school parking lot carrying an armload of papers and noticed a new shiny white Ford convertible with the top down parked on the street. Dave looked at me through dark sunglasses hiding his eyes. He didn't smile, or say hello, just sat there. Neither one of us spoke. He reached over and swung open the passenger door.

I felt nailed to the sidewalk. I must be dreaming. This was the scene I had imagined every day for months. I prayed he'd come back. And like the night he showed up at my apartment with flowers, I felt that twinge of excitement, that flutter in my stomach. He's come back. He can't let me go. He must love me.

I willed my legs to move and slipped into the passenger seat next to him. It felt natural to say nothing. Just to be with him was enough. There were no words to express my happiness. His foot hit the gas pedal and we raced away from the school. The light breeze blew my long hair into my face.

"I have something to tell you," he said.

I knew what it was. I was sure he had figured it all out during the summer. I waited. He said, "Later."

I said, "Okay, later." My heart pounded with excitement. He was going to ask me to marry him. There was no other ending to this story.

We picked up Chinese food and went to my studio apartment. We made love to each other, after months of building up the kind of intense longing, the ache of passion we always aroused in each other. Later, we sat in bed cross-legged, as we had done many times in the last year: me in bikini panties, legs still evenly suntanned from a summer of running around in shorts; he in his blue boxer shorts, still a little overweight, round sloping shoulders, smooth skin, no hair on his chest, that narrow roll of fat around his waist, and the crewcut that never suited him. We ate out of those great white Chinese takeout boxes of moo goo gai pan, shrimp with lobster sauce, egg rolls, and chow mein, using chopsticks that I was still learning to use correctly while the phonograph played Frank Sinatra singing *"All the Way."* Dave had bought me the record and scratched "I love you" on the label. We sang it together.

When somebody loves you,
It's no good unless he loves you...
All the Way–

It was "our" song. We kissed, laughed and chewed with our mouths open. We were happy. This was the moment. I couldn't wait any longer. I looked at his pale full face, not a handsome face, just a face I loved.

"So tell me."

He paused for a second, but not too long, and started to pull a photo out of his wallet. I felt panic explode in my body, like flashing red lights, sirens that screamed, "Danger, don't look!" I turned my head away.

"I'm engaged," he said, ignoring my refusal to look at the photo in his hand.

"Engaged?" I repeated, not understanding what this word meant. It was a foreign word.

"Engaged?" What did that mean? To be busy? To be working? To be studying? Engaged? To be what?

The Sinatra album was still playing, and the next record in the stack clunked as it dropped onto the turn table. The arm swung into place, stylus needle clicking onto the last record on the stack and the song began.

Fly me to the moon–

"To be married?" I finally yanked the cankerous words out of my mouth.

He was still holding the photo in his hand. He held it in front of my face and said, "Look, she's sweet, but plain-looking, not gorgeous like you."

I studied his face. Now I understood. He was expecting me to share in his joy. Was I just a good friend of his, supposed to give him a hug and say, "Be happy?" He actually wanted my blessing.

"Why?" I said.

He looked at me. I saw again the familiar sadness in the way his eyes turned down at the corners. "She thinks I'm wonderful. She sees only the good in me."

"And I don't?" No answer.

I sat quietly in bed with half-empty boxes of Chinese food spread out around me as I pictured my small kitchen counter with the cutting board knife lying there. I thought, "Get up, go into the kitchen, get the knife." I could picture its long sharp blade that I had so often cut myself with when slicing tomatoes. It was the first time in my life I had ever visualized killing someone. I imagined what it would feel like to plunge a knife into his chest, and see the blood spurt. Now I understood murder. I would kill him the way his words had killed me.

He didn't leave immediately. He wanted to make love again, like a final goodbye. I turned away to get dressed. He said, "What should I do?"

I thought the words, "Marry me," but didn't speak them. I already knew the answer. He had told me for a year all the reasons why he couldn't get married. Law school was the excuse, but I knew he didn't want me. He had given me so many clues. Why do we shut our minds to the truths when they are given to us?

He had not called after our first date. He ran away. Then on New Year's Eve, he left my apartment, saying it was his ex-wife's birthday, a brief marriage when he was eighteen in the Air Force. He said he would be too sad to spend it with me and that he needed to be alone. Yet a bouquet of thirteen roses, twelve red and one lone white one arrived at midnight. He knew how to keep me hooked. This was to become a ritual for many years, on my birthdays and sometimes New Year's Eves through the years, even when I was married. They came with no card. But I knew.

The white rose never lasted long, always faded before the others. It was ephemeral—like Dave.

I couldn't answer his "What should I do?" question. If he wanted me, he wouldn't be asking. I said sadly, "I can't tell you what to do."

I waited, but he offered nothing. He didn't say the words I was desperate to hear. He got dressed and kissed me hard, then walked out the door. I sank to the floor in the darkened room, heard the sound of his car pulling out, and then I heard the sounds of a woman sobbing, wrenching prolonged guttural wails, until retching and vomiting followed, until she was empty.

I lay on the floor all night.

I planned revenge. I would get him back and make him suffer. I would make him want me desperately. He would know this pain. I had to get him back. Then I would leave him.

I told a friend once that I had found my first "reciprocal" relationship, because we both loved each other instead of only one of us being in love with the other. Usually they were in love with me. But this time, we both loved equally—or so I thought.

It was the same fantasy I had about my father. Someday he will love me and want me. It was my brother all over again, running away from me to be with his friends when I needed him so badly, when I was so alone. The two primary men in my life had failed me. Why should this be different?

FIVE YEARS LATER, AFTER a rebound marriage to a man who could never hurt me because I didn't love him and the birth of a daughter, I landed in Arizona's dry desert and clean air with my four-year-old, Terrie. The Florida humidity had triggered severe asthma. I couldn't breathe. My husband wouldn't leave his law practice or his mother. He said I was allergic to him and would be sick wherever I went. I packed our things and got out of Florida.

In Arizona, I filed for divorce. Years later, friends remarked that I was so brave to move away with a small child all on my own. I didn't think I was brave. I had no choice. The humidity and the loveless marriage were killing me. And I was still in love with Dave.

I begged a friend to search for him. My New York friend called his law practice in Philadelphia anonymously and asked for a way to get in touch with his wife—said she was an old friend. I hoped by now he'd be divorced, too. I hoped that he would want me back.

He answered her question saying, "My wife is deceased." My poor friend was devastated. I was soon to learn of the unimaginable synchronicity of the death of his wife and baby in an automobile crash the same year, almost to the month, of my divorce. I had often wished she would die, but never his child. I didn't know there was a baby. Oh, never the baby.

Yes, I found him again. But he was shattered. He stayed alive by drinking himself into a stupor every night. I got him back. And I would never leave him. Replaying the same scene, with the same actors will result in the same ending. He always abandoned me. That was our script.

He left me in Florida, in Arizona, in San Diego, and predictably and finally, in Los Angeles. We said goodbye at airports, train stations, bus stops, and on street corners. He always said, "I love you." There were always tears in his eyes. The flowers continued to come every few years—the twelve red roses, the white one always dying first.

He said I was the sexiest woman alive and I could have anyone in the world I wanted.

"You're the only one I want," I said.

He never believed me. Many men had pursued me. I didn't want them. He was the one I couldn't have. He was the only one I wanted. Like my father, he was inaccessible. If I could make this difficult man love me, then I would believe I was lovable. Each time, I told myself that this time I would be what he wanted. I would be perfect for him. He would not send me away as my mother always threatened to do because I was a bad child. I would be good. I changed my hair color when he said he liked redheads, and wore it long because he liked it that way. I tried to do everything he asked me and was always available, always there, waiting, never leaving him, watching him drink himself into an unconscious state every night.

IN ARIZONA I TAUGHT second grade and went to school at night to get a Masters in Education at ASU, while raising a child by myself. He surfaced there for about a year, and took a separate apartment because he did not want a "family," or for Terrie to become attached to him. She did anyway. She had no other father.

He tossed her into bed at night saying, "Tuck in your head, here we go."

One night I heard her voice from the next room. "Can I call you 'Daddy'?" There was a long pause. Sitting in the kitchen I held my breath. His answer would determine my fate as well as hers.

He said, "No. I'm not used to it." That's all he said.

He would not stay with us.

I made sure he saw other men looking at me. Getting off a

train or plane, I walked next to men who would carry my bag, so that he would see me as desirable. It was a deadly game that only pushed him further away. He used to say that when we walked into a room together, all the men's heads turned to look at me. I never noticed, since I wasn't interested in anyone else's glances.

"What is that gorgeous, sexy blonde doing with that fat middle-aged Jewish man?" he would jibe. I never could convince him I loved him. I had told him I'd never love anyone else. He didn't believe me.

After he left Arizona, saying he needed to "find himself," I decided to leave the desert. I was thirty-four. Again I took my child and all our possessions and moved. I wanted a new life. I said to my Scottsdale friends, "I'm going to San Diego to get married again." And I did.

I found a teaching assignment, rented an apartment, enrolled Terrie in school and tried to forget him. I dressed up at night in sexy clothes, went to discotheques and met many men. I needed someone. I married one of the good looking, charming, younger men from the discotheque who pursued me and promised to take care of us. The marriage lasted eight months and was annulled since he was legally still married to someone else. He was a profoundly disturbed alcoholic who beat me up and threatened to kill me if I tried to leave him. I escaped with my life and no savings, which I had used to help him set up a business. He was Crazy Tom. That's how I remember and speak of him.

Near the end of this disaster in San Diego, Dave appeared again. He had driven there to see me and somehow located me at my school. We met for a drink. I told him I was married. He had a Greyhound dog in the back of his car and rented a room on the Venice Beach because the dog had become sick from driving all over the country. Dave had not "found himself" yet. I made the mistake of telling Crazy Tom that I had seen an old boyfriend for a drink. He became enraged and I paid heavily for my honesty. I had been beaten up emotionally by Dave. So being a battered wife wasn't so different. It must be what I deserved.

The annulment was easily granted.

Dave was assigned a Federal position in Los Angeles. For awhile we commuted back and forth from San Diego to L.A. Then he asked me to move there. And at the crook of his finger, I sold the house I had bought for my marriage to Crazy Tom, took a leave of absence from teaching, left friends, and gave away my cats because Dave was allergic to them. I put my furniture in storage, sent my unhappy thirteen-year-old daughter to live with a friend in New Jersey for six months. She had a daughter the same age and it bought me time to move to L.A., find a job as a School Psychologist and to be with Dave. We had three turbulent years together, most of which I spent crying in the bathroom.

HE LED ME DOWN *the steps to the sandy venice beach. I wore a bikini and no shoes.*

He liked me to look free and not carry anything, just hold his hand. I would go anywhere with this man. The sun warmed my tan skin and the pounding of the surf was like my heartbeat: happy and steady and strong. A lone girl strolling in the sand turned to look at us, and in her eyes, I saw the me that longed, was lonely, felt desolate; the look she wore on her face was a look I recognized. It was envy. And I wanted to turn to her and scream that in just a moment I would be her again. And that the bliss was fleeting and would surely be gone. I wanted to cry out: "No, you don't see this the way it really is...don't imagine that I have something you don't. It's all an illusion. There is no safety." I wanted to tell her I was alone too, that I knew abandonment, and desolation, and that this very man who looked on me now with love would no doubt leave me again, this man who held my hand so tightly would soon be gone. I wanted to tell her that this was just a moment in time. I am you, I thought. But I didn't tell. I held onto my moment in the sun.

I kept trying to please him, to make it work this time. I had to remember to buy the correct brand of fresh parmesan cheese for the gourmet Italian dinners he cooked for us. When I came back with the wrong brand of cheese, he accused me of not listening when he spoke, of not caring about him, and of not respecting and loving him.

If the hairdresser accidentally cut an inch more off the length of my hair than I asked her to, he raged that I did it on purpose because I knew how much he liked my hair, and again, that I didn't care about him. He was determined not to believe I loved him. He was impossible to please. No matter what I did to get his approval, I never did. I was never enough. Maybe Dave thought he wasn't enough for me. But I believed I was the one who was lacking. I had grown up treated as a defective. My mother tried to get rid of me too. I expected no better.

Once, I got off the elevator at the wrong floor and watched as the door closed behind me. I saw him standing inside, staring at me in disbelief. I started to laugh. It was humorous. I had made a mistake. When the elevator came back up, he didn't smile or laugh. "Why don't you pay attention? You walk around in a fog. You don't care about me at all." And then he sulked and avoided me all evening. But I kept trying for his love, trying to be good, trying not to make a mistake.

We lived in Marina Del Rey, in apartments next door to each other for a year. My daughter was back with me and he didn't want us to be a family. Then he began to put even more distance between us, and the flight pattern started again. I still closed my mind to the inevitable no matter how many times he showed me that he would never stay with me.

He moved further away to Westwood, saying it was closer to his work, which was in the Federal Building. I rushed over on Friday nights after school to spend the night with him. He made dinner, as he really enjoyed cooking. The nightly drinking ritual began around 5 p.m. I had a drink with him, usually one mixed drink, and I downed it quickly, like a soda, while he slowly and gradually consumed the full pint of what he liked to call "my boozy" throughout the night. He never recovered from the loss of his three-year-old baby. Once he let me know that he had been saving sleeping pills since the accident that killed his child. I came to believe that alcohol kept him from suicide.

"Baby, you don't know how to drink. You have to make the high last. Drink slowly." He held the half-filled glass of Jack Daniel's whiskey in his hand as he spoke, and sipped at it. But I drank my one drink, got my quick spin, and that was the end of it. It wore off. I watched as he consumed the rest of the bottle, drinking until he passed out in bed. Our evenings ended with him not knowing I was even there. I waited until morning for him to have recovered enough to reach for me.

Because he drank at night, we made love in the morning. After that, he got busy planning his day without me, putting on his white tennis shorts and shirt, lacing up the tennis shoes, a kiss, and out the door he ran, tennis bag in hand, never asking if I'd be there later. Not a word about Saturday night. Would I see him? Where would I be? He couldn't get away fast enough.

I wished I had been the one to walk out the door hurrying to my day and throwing him the kiss, having him wonder if he'd see me later. But I always let him take the lead, needing him more than he needed me. The more I tried to get it right, to be gorgeous for him, smart for him, passionate for him, the more he withdrew from me.

One night in his apartment, he told me the truth about his feelings.

"You can have any man you want. Why do you want me?" he asked, pouring himself a glass of his favorite whiskey.

"Because nobody ever wanted and needed me like you do," I said. I should have said, "Because you are the only man I can't have. Just like my father and my brother. Irresistible!"

"I don't need anyone. I know how to be alone," he said.

"You hate it," I mumbled.

Dave emptied the remains of the whiskey into the glass. He collapsed heavily into the chair holding his drink in his hand.

"I fell in love with you," I said, sitting on the floor and looking into his eyes as he tried to avoid my intense gaze.

"I never really believed that. I thought you'd find twelve more guys after me."

"I should never have told you that. I was so stupid to tell you."

"Yeah," he said. "You shouldn't have told me. It killed me." He closed his eyes as if to shut out painful images.

Oh god! The twelve red roses!

I never understood the significance of the one white rose.

I was about to find out.

In that naïve beginning twenty years earlier in Miami, I told him everything about my life, leaving nothing out, including that I had twelve sexual relationships before him. To make matters worse, I foolishly and elaborately described each one of them as he listened, rapt with interest. Why would a young stupid girl in love confess such a thing? Did I think it would add to my allure, my desirability, my worldliness?

I confessed my sins to erase the past. I thought he was my future.

"Why the thirteenth white rose?" I asked.

He didn't look at me when he said it. His head was in his hands.

"It was me. I wanted to be the last one."

"You were," I said, taking his hands away from his face and imploring him to look at me.

"Yeah, and I suppose that beautiful daughter of yours is an immaculate conception."

"You left me, remember?" I said.

"You never let me forget it."

"I knew the first time we made love that I'd never love anyone else. When you touched me, I felt something I'd never known before. It was heavenly. We fit together perfectly. I lay in your arms telling you that I loved you. Don't you remember?"

"I didn't believe you," he said. "I thought you probably always said that."

"Never." I raised my voice. "I never lied about that." I couldn't believe that for twenty years he didn't know he was the love of my life. All my friends knew it. It seemed the whole world knew it. Why didn't he know?

He said that women found his inaccessibility irresistible, that it was his most attractive trait. He was right. Dave hated his looks, and used his game plan to keep me fixated by withholding love, sex, and his physical presence in my life. It worked. I pursued him, always tempting him back into the passion we had together. He tried to escape even that. He wrapped himself in the protection of indifference and withholding, just as he wrapped himself in that blue terry cloth robe that he would sleep in with the belt wrapped around his waist twice so he was safe inside the cocoon, so that I couldn't get my hands on his body during the night. I knew about inaccessible men.

If you're a girl, and your father doesn't love you, what man will?

Thanks for Listening

I THINK WHEN ALL is said and done, the only thing that really matters is being heard.

Years of being enraged at my father didn't help me at all. In fact, it contaminated all my relationships. What did men ultimately get from me? Anger. What did I get? Gastrointestinal distress and misery. It wasn't working.

My therapist, tired of hearing me berate myself for everything I did wrong, asked me one day, "When are you going to give up your father?"

I was ticked at him for suggesting it was so easy, and under my control. Didn't he know I would if I could?

With sarcasm I snapped at him, "Next Thursday at 4:00, okay?"

The following Thursday at 4:00 (my appointment time with him) I came in and sat down on the sofa in his office.

"I pictured you dragging in your father's dead body," he said, smiling. We both laughed. But I wasn't ready to go that far. Instead I did what I needed to do all my life. Two and a half years of therapy readied me for the next encounter.

The dreaded long distance calls to my father in Florida were infrequent, no more than once a month, and mostly out of guilt. This time he called me.

"Marian, I have some CDs maturing and I want to give you $10,000," he said.

Wow! I thought. Perfect timing. I'd been dying to remodel my kitchen and get some more counter space, a decent stove with all burners working, and cover or replace those hideous, fading and peeling old walnut cabinets. I didn't have the money to consider home improvements.

"Okay, thanks, that's great," I said. This sounded good, until he put the damper on it.

"You should purchase treasury bonds with the money. I have looked into it and it's the best investment for you."

"Gee, I was thinking of getting a new kitchen," I said, sinking into a chair.

"What's wrong with your old one?" he said in that know-it-all tone I hated. "Treasury bonds is the best thing to do with the money."

I felt that old familiar queasy feeling in my stomach. I was being discredited again. He didn't hear me.

I ended the conversation and sat there seething. Damn it! He always knew better than me, and more than me. I was not an idiot. And then the anger came, red and hot. I didn't need or want his money.

The next Thursday, I saw my therapist and proudly announced that I wasn't going to take my father's money and compromise myself. "He can keep it," I said.

His response surprised me; in fact, it shocked me. I had never heard any therapist say anything like this before. He looked me in the eye and said, "Take the money. He owes you. He's the reason you're here."

This guy practically never gave me advice. It was out of

character. He was non-directive. Now he'd hit me twice with advice. Give up my father? Take his money?

The next day I called my father in Florida. I could have easily just taken the money on my father's terms and done whatever I damn well pleased with it. He never would have known. But that was not my style. I needed to do things up front. I think I secretly really needed his approval, the withheld golden egg. The money was not what I needed from him. I desperately longed for his respect, his love? Well, don't ask for too much.

"Okay, Dad," I said, warming up to what I was about to say. "I need you to listen." I was near the wall phone and had decided to do this standing up. I did not want to be relaxed. It was quiet on the other end of the line.

I began, "All of my life you have discounted my abilities and made me feel inadequate."

He started to interrupt. "Oh, Marian...it's okay...do what you want with the money." He wanted to shut me up.

"No!" I shouted into the phone. "I need to say this. And I need you to just listen."

He began to argue with me. "You can spend the money any way you want—"

Now I yelled at the top of my lungs, something I never had the courage to do with my father. I never yelled at him. Never.

"I NEED YOU TO JUST LISTEN!" My voice was strong. That alone felt good, a relief. I needed him there on the phone... hearing me.

"Don't hang up," I thought. Just stay there and hear this. I need to say it. I must say it.

I continued to stand there, gripping the phone. Again it was quiet on his end of the line. I continued, "I grew up thinking I did everything wrong, was dumb, incompetent. The way you treated me damaged my perception of myself. It ruined all my relationships with men." I took a breath.

He tried once more to stop me. But I shouted right over him. I was not crying, the way I usually did when I had to face my father. Strangely enough, I wasn't angry either. I was just by god going to say what I wanted to say for the first time in my life.

I felt a surge of energy firing through my body and heard a voice that was not fearful coming out of me. It was forceful and direct. It was also passionate and emotional. Years of saving this up exploded as I told him the rest.

"I want you to know," I continued, "that I have lived a courageous and competent life. I have achieved successes professionally, raised a child alone, managed everything on my own, with no help from anyone. I have not asked you for anything. And I have handled money wisely and safely. I have never been irresponsible in my life."

It felt so good to be saying this. It was the truth. I realized I was telling myself as well as my father. These were the things I didn't believe. And now, here they were.

I went right on, "And most of all, I want you to know I am capable of handling money, and making good decisions about spending and saving. I am worthy of respect. I am worth trusting. And when you suggest that you know better about how I should handle gift money, it is the same thing I've experienced my whole life. It says I'm incompetent."

Now there was dead silence on the line. I was on a roll. I couldn't stop.

"So, Dad, if there is anything that I am, it is competent. And if this money is a gift, then I say thank you. But if it comes with a tag that says, 'You're too dumb to know what to do with this', then I can't take it."

I was finished. My breathing was even and calm. There was

no sound except my breath. I hoped he was still on the phone and that I hadn't given him a stroke or heart attack.

"You still there?" I said.

His voice was small. "I know I wasn't the perfect father." He had never denied being perfect before. This was huge. Was this the man I had been so frightened of? "I did the best I could," he said.

Now I felt empowered and forgiving.

"Dad, I'm not asking you to change. I was only asking you to just listen. I didn't tell you this to make you feel bad or to be different than you are. I needed just to be heard. I needed *you* to hear me. And you did."

"Okay," he said, in a resigned voice.

"Thank you," I said. "Thank you for letting me say what I needed to say. Thank you for listening. That's everything."

"I'll put the check in the mail today," he said. "Enjoy your kitchen."

"Thanks, I will."

On the following Thursday I came into my shrink's office and grinned at him.

"What happened?" he asked.

I told him the whole thing.

His face lit up. "Well, now you have a father," he said.

"No," I corrected him. With all his degrees in clinical psych, he was wrong in his assessment of this. "It's too late," I said. "I needed a father for many years, all my life. But not now. It's over."

My therapist looked surprised and a little disappointed. He liked happy endings. But I knew you can't have what you didn't get.

I wrote my dad a thank you note. It wasn't for the $10,000 check that arrived that day. It said, "Thanks for listening. You gave me what I needed."

Yet, before he died, he gave me what I needed a thousand times more than being heard. I couldn't have planned it or asked for it. It was simply given which is the only true value of a gift. He was 99 years old, and planning to live to his own projected date of one hundred years, which he did. I visited him in Florida in a rehab facility. I remember walking into the room and seeing an old man sleeping peacefully in the hospital bed. His face was thinner, but he looked like my father; same bald head, a few white hairs around the rim of his skull. Yes, it was him. I came closer to the bed and sat down in the chair to wait for him to waken.

He must have sensed my presence as he opened his eyes and looked right at me. And then he did something I'd never seen him do before. As he registered recognition, his face lit up with delight, a huge smile as he said my name. "Marian."

He was happy to see me. I had never seen that before. I was shocked. I couldn't believe the joy that registered on his face because I was there. I smiled back. "Hi, Dad." Who was this man? Was this the father I thought never liked me? Did he know he was dying and these were his true feelings? How sad that he waited so many years to light up when he looked at me. But at least I had seen it once in my life. When a parent loves a child and his face lights up whenever the child appears, the child knows it, feels it. I only saw the scowling, the "what did you do wrong today?" face. I never saw joy in my father's face when he looked into mine. I was more stunned than happy. We could have had a relationship. We never did. "He is smiling at me now," I thought.

He died in his sleep a few months later, right after his one hundredth birthday. I heard that he bragged about it. "I'm a hundred, you know."

I think he died happy. I forgave him, and myself. Neither of us were perfect.

Epilogue to a Funeral

I THROW A SHOVEL full of gritty sand—allegedly from Israel—on his coffin and watch in disbelief as the long gray box is lowered in slow motion next to my mother's gravesite, going down, slowly, slowly. I say the words silently to myself, embarrassed by them, "Goodbye, Daddy." In my peripheral vision, I catch the splendid sight of a squirrel in the grass standing up on his back paws about twenty feet away. I feel the corners of my mouth turn up into an unplanned reflexive smile and turn away from the coffin to watch.

The furry little creature stands upright, facing the ceremony as if to witness this moment. His paws are wrapped around something he holds onto tightly, his glorious bushy tail curled around him on the ground. I stare; coffin still going down in slow motion. But I cannot take my eyes away from the squirrel. Suddenly, two groundsmen wearing park green uniforms approach him. I'm afraid. Please—no—I pray. Let him stay. I need him here.

One of the men reaches into his shirt pocket. I stop breathing. The animal freezes in his spot, not moving or running away, still standing up attentively. Tears roll down my face and the smile fades. I think that they are going to poison or injure my squirrel. The man takes out a small orange square wrapped in cellophane, carefully unwraps it, and hands it directly to the little guy, who takes it rapidly and begins munching on it. It looks like one of those peanut butter cracker sandwiches from a candy dispenser. I exhale gratefully. My squirrel is alive and well and being cared for. When I turn back to the coffin, it is disappearing deep into the opening in the ground. I think, "Dad's gone." The words that come to me now are the ones given to Jeff Goldblum in the film *Jurassic Park*, words used to predict the uncanny survival of dinosaurs unable to reproduce. "Life will find a way" is the line. It struck me at the time and has stayed in the part of my brain that stores my forever words.

I see my relatives getting into their cars, starting up the engines, everyone rushing madly to get away from coffins in the earth, and illness and dying and all of our relentless futures, rushing away, going where? If they hurry they can get there sooner.

I hear my name being called, but I'm on my way over to the groundsman, for there lies my solace, not in the car with my family.

I tell him, "I saw you feeding the squirrel, as we buried my father."

He smiles. "We feed them all the time."

I feel a need to acknowledge this man, his nurturing, his significance in the universe. I blurt out some words about the profound sense of completion he has given me today. Then I tell the rabbi who stands quietly nearby, still holding his little black prayer book, having just completed in Hebrew the prayer for the dead.

I say excitedly, "Did you see the squirrel?" This is important. I search his clear eyes waiting for validation. Will he understand? In the distance I hear them calling me. The rabbi takes my hand and holds it as he gives me the words I need to keep in my heart. He says exquisitely, "Yes. It is a sign."

Gratitude

WHILE READING PHIL MCGRAW'S *Ten Life Strategies*, the exercises asked me to list the ten most important people in my life and write down what would be left unsaid if one of us died. I am one of those readers who do all exercises required. When I read Julia Cameron's *The Artist's Way* I did whatever she said to do. I am a good and obedient reader.

So I wrote the messages to ten people. Nine of the people were living, and I was able to send them their messages. The tenth person was my father. He never got this one.

AFTER I COMPLETED MY last trip to Florida to his grave, I thought I'd better tell him. In Jewish tradition, there is an "unveiling" of the tombstone a year after the funeral and burial. It is a sacred ceremony led by a rabbi. My brother and I were called up to stand together at the gravesite as the rabbi said the Hebrew prayers.

My brother's wife stood apart. I always felt she took him away from me. Now for a few moments he was mine. It was clear. It was about us, the two children of Herman. No one could break this bond. We instinctively held hands at our father's grave, like two children. This was the brother I had lost. Now we were together to say goodbye to our father, the father I thought loved him more. We were connected as we had been as children.

The tears rolled down my face and I felt joy. My father was gone and we were children saying goodbye to him. Rob held my hand as he had so many times when taking me to school. He was my big brother. I was his little sister even though I was three inches taller than he was.

This is the letter I wrote to my father.

Dad: I know you did your very best. I know you never meant to do me harm. I never told you of the gifts you provided for me. Because of you I am a responsible person, reliable and loyal to my friends. Because of you I have a sense of ethics, and am effective in the things I choose to do. Because of you, I know how to manage money, stay out of debt, save and spend wisely. I am grateful to you for sharing your values. I know the value of saving, turning lights off in each room I leave, not being foolish in handling money, never borrowing money, never becoming dependent on others for things I can do for myself, wearing slippers in the house, taking care of things that need care, taking care of people who need care. Because of you I know how to save for the larger things I want; I also know how to wait for what I want, and never squander money, and save wisely. I also know how to purchase the best tickets in the theatre and eat at the best restaurants. These things I learned from you.

I never thanked you for the care and concern you always gave me, getting up out of a warm bed after working long nights to drive me to school if it was snowing or raining, buying me coloring books in an effort to get me to eat, coming around to my bedroom every night to pour water into the pan that hung on the radiator so there would be moisture in my bedroom. I know now that you would have thrown yourself in front of a moving train to save me. I've spent so much time being angry at you for the things you didn't give me that I never thanked you for the things you did give. I know now that you loved me. Thanks, Dad.

PART III

HOLLY GO LIGHTLY

"Go Say Hello"

LYING IN THE CORNER on a sheepskin pad, Holly Go Lightly waits. Her mouth is curved in that famous Golden Retriever grin; her tail thumps the floor in anticipation while she holds the "down-stay" position, waiting for her signal to go to work.

Nearby, elderly patients sit in chairs placed in a circle. They also wait, some without purpose, others simply waiting to die. There is no conversation. Some of the patients look confused, as if they don't know where they are; others mumble to themselves. One man is slumped over half-asleep, perhaps medicated. The atmosphere in the room is heavy with the depression that comes with Alzheimer's, dementia, and other psychiatric disorders. We are in the Neuro-Psychiatric Hospital at UCLA's Medical Center.

Vigilant, Holly watches me. She sits sphinx-like on all fours, head up, ears forward and alert, watching and listening for her cue. I point to the patients, and give her the release words, "Go say hello." In a flash, she's up, her tail swaying gracefully as she trots to the circle of chairs, moving through the one space we have left open for her. She moves to the center of the group, stops and appears to be scanning the room. Someone is in distress.

Arms thrashing, his body writhes in the hospital chair while his moans and groans are heard over the mumblings of the other patients. Holly moves deliberately to the side of the agitated gentleman, stands by him for a moment, and then lays her head in his lap. From deep in the animal's throat there is a low vibrating note that sounds like "Ummmmm."

Alfred Langer, a ninety-year-old Alzheimer's patient, has not communicated with anyone in the three months he's been in residential care. He has been unreachable, to quote one of the therapists in *Senior Rehab*. Holly continues to hum her throaty mantra, while Alfred's vocalizations noticeably change volume and tone to match hers. Together they hum, "Ummm, ummmm." The old man's body becomes still. His arms relax. Now, one hand reaches slowly to touch the golden head in his lap as they sing their song together.

Holly doesn't move from his side, but lifts her head to stare into his eyes. Alfred returns her gaze, regarding her calmly. He releases the rigid tension that has held him captive.

There is a hush in the room. One of the nurses wipes a tear from her eyes. The staff as well as the patients sit still and silent in what can only be described as reverence. All who are present are in awe of what they just witnessed—the power of Animal-Assisted Therapy, the healing without medication, without sedation, without restraints.

My canine partner had sensed agitation in the room. I learned not to interfere with her process by talking to her or giving her cues while she is assessing a group. I let her nose do its work. This is her best sensory tool. It is instinctual. And it is powerful. The extraordinary canine sense of smell enables dogs to diagnose depression, anxiety, disorientation, and psychiatric disorders through being alert to chemical changes in the body. They sense crisis the same way medical-alert dogs predict seizures and heart attacks, detect breast and bladder cancers, and warn diabetics of low blood sugar. They smell it!

With Alfred Langer sitting calmly, Holly prepares to help her next patient. She moves in a clockwise direction, stopping in front of a woman who is clutching her leather bag in her lap. The patient's name tag reads Lila. Her mouth is downturned and her lips pursed tightly. Frown lines run deep between her eyes. The dog sits in front of her, then lifts a paw and offers it as she makes eye contact with the woman. Lila hesitates as Holly continues to wave her paw in the air. Finally the woman takes hold of it, shakes it, and says, "Hello." I notice the frown lines soften on her face and her mouth starts to smile as she releases the handshake and reaches out to touch the dog's soft head.

Holly doesn't skip anyone in the circle. She stops to greet each person, waiting long enough to get a response from them, before moving on. She is here to communicate with those who are disconnected from themselves and from life. She will not leave them until she makes that connection.

The next patient is asleep. Holly stands alongside his chair staring at him, just as she stares at closed doors waiting for them to open magically for her. Maybe he hears her breathing, or feels her presence in the same instinctive way that we know when someone is watching us. He opens his eyes to see a dog looking at him. He appears confused as to what to do about it, until she lifts her paw and puts it into his lap. From somewhere in his memory, he recognizes the gesture, and takes the extended paw in his hand. With his free hand, he touches the top of her head, and whispers, "Good dog." Even when memory is impaired, some things are never forgotten.

Holly will approach the person in need: the suicidal kid, the withdrawn adult, or the wildly agitated Alzheimer's patient. She will look into his eyes, offer her paw, or lean into his body. She will stay with each patient until her presence is acknowledged. She will wait, not moving from the spot until a hand reaches out to touch her.

I watch as my dog raises her paw, offering it to the next patient in the circle. I feel a warm rush in my body, a glow of pride. Holly is my working partner. Her strength is my strength. She and I did this together. This is the reason we are here. This is the purpose that Holly has brought to my life.

THE TRUTH IS THAT none of this could have happened just this way without beginning just the way it did.

The Search for Perfection

I GLARED AT THE white phone mounted on the kitchen wall as if my intention would make it ring. It had been six weeks since eleven Golden Retriever puppies were removed by C-section from Brightly, the Golden mother of the litter. I had anxiously waited for the results of the routine six week evaluation to determine which puppies had *show quality*. The ones that met the breed's conformation standards would go to homes wanting show dogs. The others would be sold as pets.

The phone finally rang and I heard the excited voice of Karla, the breeder. "I have your Holly," she said, "and she's not show quality."

I should have been thrilled. I had asked for pet quality. "Oh god," I mumbled, "what's wrong with her?" I pictured a puppy with crossed eyes, or one ear lop-sided, or some terrible fault that would eliminate her from show dog potential.

"Nothing," said Karla. "She's perfect."

"Really?" I felt my clammy hands holding the phone. I never get anything perfect.

For a year, I drove all over California, visited kennels and met breeders in my search for the perfect puppy. I wanted a Golden Retriever with a pedigree of good health, good temperament and great looks. A well-known breeder in California recommended the unborn litter of two champions. I reviewed their portfolios and health histories. The Dam was Brightly, a champion whose soft head and blonde beauty stole my heart, and the Sire was Kirby (registered name Haagan Das, like the ice cream), a reddish-colored, sporty-looking retriever, grand champion in the U.S. and Canada, loved by the judges because of his elegant stance and calm temperament.

I signed a contract with the breeder requesting a "pet quality bitch" (this is not sarcasm, just breeder jargon). Even though the sire and dam were both champions, I was not looking for a show dog. I didn't want to be without her on weekends while she was being shown all over the country, traveling with a handler to dog shows. I simply wanted the puppy I was never allowed as a child for cuddling, to lick my face, comfort me, listen to my troubles and be my loyal best friend. But I needed her to be perfect. I was the defective child. At least let my dog be okay.

"We measured her forechest, and it's a little too narrow for conformation standards. Champions have deep, wide, well developed chests," she explained.

I exhaled the tension I was holding in and said, "Thank you, god." She will never make champion. She will never be best in show. I will never have to lose her to the show world. She was perfect for me.

The next day I was in the car driving north to have a look at the new litter. I was going to meet the dog I had dreamed of since I was seven. I stuffed my mouth with potato chips, Snickers bars, and other junk foods while driving 80 miles an hour up Highway 101. I arrived in Cotati, California, a small town just north of San

Francisco, checked into a Holiday Inn, and called the breeder. "It's late," she told me. "Come tomorrow." All night I visualized hundreds of Golden Retriever puppies leaping over hurdles, like sheep jumping fences. But I was wide awake. The next morning, alert, living on adrenalin, I followed the directions the breeder gave me, driving slowly up the street looking at house numbers. Then I saw them.

On a front lawn, a wire pen encircled what looked like ten piglets with the sun lighting them up as if on a stage with spotlights. As I drove closer, I determined they weren't piglets at all, but chubby, furry, roly-poly Golden puppies. With little black noses and floppy golden ears, they romped in the grass, rolling over each other, some sitting up on their haunches looking at me. One wandered off and was trying to dig his way out of the pen, nose to the ground, blades of grass flying. Another one pounced in a rocking horse motion with legs uncoordinated, climbing through the crowd of fat little bodies, giving a short yip before losing his balance and falling over. He got up, shook himself off and started his romp all over again. I realized I was holding my breath. They were beautiful. All of them. I looked at the glitter of Golden puppies sparkling in the sunlight as I sat in the car crying.

Later, sitting on the grass in the playpen, I let ten pups climb all over me. "Don't tell me which one is Holly. Not yet," I said to the breeder/owner. Professional breeders choose the puppies for you, matching your needs and life style to the animal. I was really afraid she wouldn't be the best one. I picked up and held the fattest little fellow with his rotund tummy, full blonde coat and the sweetest square-shaped face, by far the cutest one in the litter.

"Can I have this one?" I asked the breeder, already knowing the answer.

She laughed. "You have good taste. He's the male pick of the litter. He'll go to a show home, he's promised to the co-breeder."

Sitting quietly watching the others was a smaller, less full-coated, thinner little pup. I noticed her.

"Oh," afraid to ask. "Which one is Holly?"

"That one," the breeder pointed. She was the one in the corner by herself. My face dropped. I bent down and picked her up. She was not the prettiest puppy by a long shot. I was told I could take her home with me. She was only six weeks old. Putting her down on the grass, I watched her run over to a rather worn out-looking adult Golden, and standing underneath the large dog, tilt her head up. Oh my god! She was nursing. I aimed my Instamatic camera at them, realizing she was not going home with me that day. She needed her mother.

I drove back to L.A. with no dog in the car, tears in my eyes, and feeling disappointment because she was not the perfect dog I had hoped for. She actually looked a little "runty." Nothing I had was ever good enough. Friends assured me that she would probably fill out and look better by the time she was shipped by plane to me in a couple of weeks. I accepted the fact that she wasn't the gorgeous puppy I wanted. I would make the best of it. I got busy arranging the house with the necessary supplies, puppy food, squeaky toys, stuffed animals, soft sheepskin pads, and a green flowered comforter for a dog bed. I installed a pet door to an upstairs patio so she could sit out in the sun and watch the world go by. What more was there to do? I didn't yet have a clue.

ONE WEEK AND THREE days later, I waited nervously at the Los Angeles airport in a small receiving room outside of the baggage claim area. At seven and a half weeks, probably still too young to be separated from her mother and littermates, Holly arrived. I was incapable of waiting the recommended three weeks longer that all the books suggest. The sooner I got her, the sooner we could begin the bonding, the hugs and kisses I'd been saving up for the last fifty years of my life.

Two friends came with me so that I could hold my new 'baby' in my arms on the way home. My next-door neighbor and friend, Karen, had actually thrown me a 'puppy shower' weeks before. Slung over her arm, she carried a handmade patchwork receiving blanket that her mother Emma had made. This was a dog, not a baby. We were all a little nuts. Jean, who had spent the last thirty years of her life rescuing animals, brought along the flashbulb camera that accompanied her everywhere. She had forgiven me for not adopting one of her needy rescues.

Finally, double doors swung open and an airport attendant carrying a small kennel crate stepped through. My mouth gaped and I sucked in my breath. He asked, "Is this yours?" I stared at the box he was holding unable to move or speak. Taking the receipt I was clutching in my damp hand, he matched the numbers with those posted on the crate. "Yes ma'am" he said smiling. "Here's your puppy." My knees felt weak. This was the moment I had longed for since I was a child. I thought my legs would buckle. Karen and Jean grabbed onto my hands to keep me upright. The attendant set the crate down and asked me to sign some papers. I scribbled my name. Then I got down on my knees and peered between the metal bars. My eyes met a pair of almond shaped black eyes, wide open and alert. The Golden Retriever puppy was sitting up and looking all around. Her jet black nose sat on the tip of a blonde muzzle. Her head was nearly white, with a small oval at the top (Golden enthusiasts call it the 'smart bump'). The puppy was very quiet, just watching us. She was calm. There was no barking or whimpering. She had filled out and wasn't "runty." In fact, she was beautiful. And I was in love.

I scrambled to get her out of the crate she'd been confined in all the way from Northern California to LAX. I felt the bedding, all dry. I picked her up, wrapped her in that silly receiving blanket which I called her "blankie" and cuddled her in my arms like a newborn infant. I covered her face and head with kisses. Her coat felt as soft as the silky feathers of the canaries of my childhood, and she had a special sweet breath, that I was told is puppy breath.

The one thing I wanted more than anything was a puppy with a good temperament. Since I had failed in all my love relationships, making the right connection with this dog was crucial to my redemption. I would do everything right. I would have the best dog. *It was safe to love again.*

I had been reading Roger Caras' Dog Book to determine the best breed for me; The Monks of New Skete on training; and several books on obedience training and behavior. I went to dog shows, talked to breeders and owners and educated myself about this breed for over a year. With all of this research, I still didn't know what I was doing. I never had a dog in my life. I never held a leash.

Cameras flashed. My friends were recording this moment for me. The wet little tongue licked my face. I closed my eyes and felt heaven in my arms. Then, remembering my friends who were nearly drooling by now, I gently handed her to Karen and then Jean (the aunties) and she licked each of their faces too. I looked her over. In contrast to her light coloring, her floppy ears were the color of honey. This is the color she would become, a reddish gold color that was now being hinted at with splashes on her back and feet. Her paws were large, accented by perfect little black nails. I believed I would have her all to myself. I thought I could be a good dog mom. I expected to be happy. I was wrong, on all counts.

Recalling my thoughts on this first day with Holly, I thought I was her mother, and she was my new baby—a canine baby. How delightful! Yes, there really had been a puppy shower. They had even made me wear a pillow under my loose shirt that day. Were we all crazy? That was my first shower ever. I had never been given a bridal shower or a baby shower. I had never even been to a prom. I had a wedding ceremony but was never any good at being married, had tried it twice. In fact I was not good at relationships. I was divorced, lived alone, had one adult child and always longed for another baby. Here it was.

What I really needed was another chance to be good.

Bad Dog

I ALWAYS THOUGHT THERE were naturally aggressive breeds: Pit Bulls, Rottweilers, Mastiffs, Chows, German Shepherds, Dobermans, and other dogs that are bred for dominance and protection. I was careful not to choose one of these. I chose the Golden Retriever, known for its gentle and sweet temperament, a dog whose purpose is to retrieve and carry things in his mouth, not to bite. I never dreamed that aggression can be displayed in any breed if the dog becomes unstable.

At the age of three months, Holly became a victim of dog attacks. The first incident occurred when we were visiting my neighbor, and Holly apparently made the mistake of standing too near the water dish of the resident Cocker Spaniel. He lunged at her face with his teeth, and tore the skin around her eye. Holly yelped in that high-pitched puppy squeal that usually sounds worse than it is. I ran over, bent down, and saw blood seeping from a wound under her eye. I picked her up, and together my neighbor and I cleaned the wound and put Neosporin on it, all the while cuddling and cooing to her sympathetically. I carried her home, concerned that she would have a scar on her perfect face. After that, wherever we went, she seemed to attract aggression. I didn't know why this kept happening to my sweet, friendly puppy. I must be doing something wrong. It had to be my fault. I worried, tightening the lead whenever a new dog was in sight. I must have telegraphed that tension through the leash. Holly was reflecting my fear. And so it kept happening.

We were out for a walk one evening and stopped to chat with Richard and Barbara, some neighbors. Richard's German Shepherd Rex was twelve years old and stood next to him eyeing my puppy. As we were visiting, Rex suddenly lunged at Holly, teeth snapping at her eye. Richard yanked him back on his leash and said too softly, it seemed to me, "Rex, no."

I screamed, "No!" and bent down. Blood was flowing from her right eye. Her lid was ripped open. "Oh my god," I thought. "She's lost her eye."

"Marian, don't worry, I'll pay for the veterinary bills." Richard was still holding onto his dog.

I snapped at him, "I don't want veterinary expenses, I don't want her hurt."

Why didn't he have control over his dog? I was to learn that this dog had a history of ripping open eyelids of other dogs in the neighborhood. That was his modus operandi. What an idiot! He saw that I had a puppy. Why didn't he warn me? I carried her home bleeding and crying (both of us). This was the second attack.

There was a third incident in the park. When she was four months old I was talking with a trainer, considering taking some obedience classes from her. Her black lab stood nearby watching us. All at once, he lunged at Holly, clamping his teeth down on her nose. She screamed and ran away, yelping. I ran after her, my body shaking, unable to believe this nightmare kept repeating itself. I again collected her as she shook and whined in my arms. I comforted her with affection, thinking this was the correct thing to do. I had no idea I was rewarding her for being afraid, simply because I was. I had no idea I was teaching her to stay frightened.

The pigment was ripped off Holly's black nose. It stayed pink for months, to my utter despair. My perfect puppy was being marred, a piece at a time. She was becoming physically scarred, and I became afraid to leave the house for fear of another attack

At five months, there was a final incident when we were in the park. Two large mixed breeds were loose, running around with no owner in sight. They loped over to check her out. She let out a fierce warning growl and showed them her canine teeth in a grimace. They leaped on her, snapping and snarling. I couldn't separate them and I screamed for help. I thought they would kill her. She was fighting back and it looked like she was fighting for her life, with snarls, teeth bared, bodies twisting. I couldn't pull her away. I tried kicking them, but I felt helpless, and they never took me seriously. It seemed like forever until a woman came running over to call her dogs off.

"You need to keep your dogs with you!" I told her. I was shaking. Holly was shaking too. Miraculously she was frightened, but not injured.

She was not provoking or aggressing. She was a "victim" as clearly as if it were written on her forehead. All I wanted to do was protect her. So I avoided other dogs. Protecting her, of course, was the worst thing I could have done. This did not build confidence. I learned, too late, that dogs look for other confident dogs to connect with. The pack members must be strong. Wolves living in packs run from or attack weakness in pack members in order for the pack to survive. Holly was attracting aggression now because the dogs sensed her weaknesses, probably in much the same way that I had attracted the wrong men into my life. Through the study of wolf packs and their behavior, I came to understand what had happened to my dog. I saw the parallels to my own life. I had attracted the wrong men into my life with my lack of self-worth. My fear and weakness were magnets for abusive treatment. I had not learned to stand up for myself. Neither had Holly. We were alike. But she was about to turn that around and fight for her own safety.

Like children of repeated abuse, she learned to use defensive aggression to protect herself, as if to say "victim no more." By the time she was a year old, it was she who started displaying full-blown aggression whenever we passed a strange dog on the street. "Get them before they get you" seemed to be her motto. I could barely hang onto her or restrain her. She would rear up on her hind legs, revealing canine teeth in a grimace that I called her "wolf face." The change was dramatic; I did not recognize my sweet, gentle Golden Retriever who loved everyone. In fact, she scared me.

She smelled my fear and became unstable, fearful, and more aggressive with unknown dogs. I had been through all the dog trainers, all the devices, read all the books, and had not been able to extinguish her deep fear and distrust. My friend Nina, a dog trainer, taught me to throw her over on her side and pin her to the ground when she aggressed. I wasn't very good at it; she was strong and resisted going down. She snarled at me if I tried to dominate her.

Nina also taught me to use a kennel lead high up on her neck and "hang" her by tightening it to control these outbursts every time we saw a new dog. Although she never bit any of them, and I suspect it was all bravado, I worried she would threaten the wrong dog, and that one day they would kill her. I lived in fear of losing her. And worse than that. It would be my fault.

When she acted aggressively, she became the pack leader, the one in charge. She was taking responsibility for the pack safety instead of me. She would growl if she sensed danger. I had an unstable dog because she really needed a leader; in fact, she required a leader to stay balanced. But she didn't have one. If I tried to interfere or correct her, the snarls and threatening postures were turned directly on me.

I often went home and cried, or needed a drink, or both. I felt betrayed by this dog that I adored. How could she turn on me?

"For two dollars I'll sell her to the gypsies," I joked with friends about Holly while she was right there at my feet. It was the same abandonment I'd felt as a child when my mother threatened to sell me to the gypsies. To my horror, years of feeling weak and disrespected throughout my life were being replayed in the dynamics of this relationship. My wonderful Holly Go Lightly was a bad dog. My worst nightmare was coming true. She was like me.

AND NOW, SO MANY years later, far away from my misdirected and confused family, I was still fearful after every incident of aggression with Holly. I consulted with dog trainers, went to workshops, tried every aversive means to stop aggression: prong collar, choke chain, Halti lead over the muzzle. I was reluctantly considering an electronic collar that would deliver a low-frequency jolt as correction. I tried every device—except me.

AND THEN SOMETHING HAPPENED to change the course of this journey with my dog.

Dr. Holly

EARLY ONE MORNING, WHILE strolling across the grassy knoll just outside of my condo, my eight-month-old puppy in tow, I felt a determined tug on the lead and let it go, releasing the dog to follow her instincts. Walking toward us were my neighbors, Mabel and Jorge, an Argentine couple. "Go say hello," I said, pretending it was my idea when it was clearly hers. I barely knew this couple other than to nod hello in the parking garage. But that was about to change. Holly trotted over to them as if they were family and they responded by bending down to greet her with open arms, welcoming the adorable puppy who ran to them with a rocking horse gait, legs uncoordinated, tail waving. She leaned against Mabel, held her front paw in the air, and looked into the woman's eyes. She did the same with Jorge. They both melted. "Ah, she's a sweetheart" said Mabel, taking the extended paw into her own hand like a handshake. Her husband knelt down and petted Holly's head. Not only had my dog made a connection, she had offered me one as well.

This was a phenomenon that would change my life. I rarely reached out to new people, yet these two neighbors and dozens of others were to become my friends through Holly's irresistible friendliness. There was no avoiding it. The world opened for me.

I had a dog who was more interested in meeting people than in taking a walk. She pranced gracefully to anyone in her path, tail swaying, ears flopping, mouth open in a curved smile with her pink tongue visible. Some people were surprised at the enthusiasm with which she greeted them. Yet she was polite and respectful. She didn't jump all over them as some puppies do; she went over and sat down as if to introduce herself. Although she sometimes waved a paw in the air, she always gazed into their eyes. People we had never met before would tenderly touch her head, stroke her back, and admire her. Some would say, "I'm not really into dogs, but this one I like," or "There is something special about her." I heard myself saying "thank you" as if they were complimenting me. Everyone she met responded to her. I glowed with a pride I had never felt before. I was getting approval through this dog. I had searched for approval all my life. This was unexpected.

And with it came the realization that I had a canine therapist on a leash. She was not here just to meet my emotional longings for the dog I was denied. Holly had come bearing many gifts. She would change lives. She would change mine.

I felt a responsibility to find an environment in which to return the gifts. I knew I had to put her together with those that needed her. I was already one of them.

I had heard about therapy dogs that worked in hospitals and clinics. I suspected I had one of those standing right in front of me. Although I didn't know it yet, she already had the skills to do this work. "Go say hello'" would become the cue words to do what she loved: connect with people.

Holly looked directly into the eyes of strangers, and they were drawn to shake the paw she held poised in mid-air. "How did you teach her to do this?" was the question I heard most often. "I didn't teach her," I said. "She came this way."

Having been a Family Therapist and School Psychologist for

twenty years, I understood only too well that the world was desperately in need of healing. When I saw that Holly made direct eye contact with every human she met, my mind raced with the possibilities. This dog eagerly gazed into the eyes of each person, bringing them back into the present moment and its honesty. Her penetrating gaze and probing eyes touched people and appeared to lift their spirits. All of my experience and instincts told me I was witnessing a therapeutic connection. I couldn't ignore it.

I announced to my daughter that Holly was going to be a therapy dog. Terrie replied, "Is that what *she* wants to do?" My answer was that it was *she* who had told *me*. Although I was confident about her mission, we were about to enter uncharted waters. I knew nothing about therapy animals. I had wanted a companion, not a working dog. I ignored the aggression with strange new dogs and focused on creating something positive. This dog would save us both.

After procrastinating for months and asking dog trainers where to locate a facility offering a pet therapy program, I finally found the courage to call the Huntington Memorial Hospital in Pasadena. I had been told they had a Pet Assisted Therapy Program (PAT). I spoke with the director, offered to volunteer, and thought it was a good sign when she told me her name was Holly. It was she who suggested that Pasadena was a long drive from my home in Culver City and that UCLA might be starting a program soon. This time I did not wait. I called the medical center immediately and spoke to the nursing administrator, proclaiming that my dog had *special gifts*. I threw in that I held professional licenses in the therapy field as well. We were both qualified. I'm sure that was overkill, as they were looking for volunteers, not professionals, but I needed her to say yes. She exclaimed, "Oh my god, we were just this week approved to begin a program using dogs and we were wondering where to find them. The angels must have dropped you from heaven." I hung up the phone and threw my arms into the air yelling, "Yes!"

The next morning, I dressed quickly and nervously, taking time to put on eye liner and blush so I wouldn't look as if I hadn't slept all night. I drove to UCLA with a very clean ten-month-old puppy lying on towels in the back seat of my Camry. She had been shampooed, her teeth brushed with her own electric toothbrush, and her outer ears cleaned gently with cotton balls. She was groomed until there was not a single tangle in her reddish golden coat. Something was about to happen. She watched me attentively.

We climbed four levels of fire exit stairs from the dark C level underground parking facility and emerged into the bright sunlight of the Plaza Level. I spotted two women standing in front of the Medical Center. It was a clear day and the main building was flanked by well-manicured green grass that sparkled in the sun. We respectfully walked around the large grassy area, staying on the paved pathways as we approached the hospital. I was excited, and Holly, feeling my high spirits, trotted along happily beside me, tail waving like a flag in the breeze.

The Administrator of Nursing Services, with whom I had spoken, was waiting there to greet us. We shook hands and she introduced me to Kc Cole, a cardiac nurse who said a brief hello to me, then got down on her knees in the grass and petted and hugged my puppy. Holly did not hesitate at this invitation to play, and nuzzled Kc, who laughed and nuzzled her back. This affectionate display surprised me because I had come expecting a formal interview, or evaluation. Then I realized: *this was it*. Kc and Holly were all over each other like two puppies. The administrator, on the other hand, was more reserved. She stood back and commented, "He's frisky, isn't he?" This alarmed me. Was she too active to do this kind of work? Holly was always considered to be calm for a puppy, and she was still under a year old. I learned that Anna was the supportive administrator who mentored the inception of the program. But it turned out that Kc was the "animal person" who would soon be director of the brand new People-Animal Connection Program (PAC). The two fell in love with each other from that first romp in the grass. They formed a bond that lasted to the last day of Holly's life, when Kc came to say goodbye.

I learned in the years to come that Holly was not unique in her feelings for Kc. Every PAC dog fell in love with her. The honest way she greeted them with no false notes, the eye contact she made with them, and her non-verbal approach created instant mutual trust. And they never forgot who she was. Trust the dogs to know.

During the years we worked in the hospital, although she was trained not to pull on her lead and always walked respectfully by my side or behind me, when Holly heard the magic words, "Let's go see Auntie Kc," her ears perked up, and her tail wagged fiercely. She would drag me down the center hallway, past the information desk and head straight to the PAC office where she would stand facing the door, knowing Kc was on the other side. Once in the room, Holly and Kc would collapse in a heap of human and canine limbs. These encounters were physical and non-verbal, and this is the way dogs meet each other.

Often at meetings and parties, I offered a tribute that "dog people" recognize as the ultimate praise. I would say, "No pack in the wild survives without a leader. In the PAC program, Kc is our alpha dog."

As the only volunteer team in the program, Kc gave us a private orientation to hospital protocol. The first step was to introduce Holly to the Cardiac Care Unit (CCU) without patient visits. The plan was to walk her through the rooms and hallways and show her this new environment. Having never been in a hospital before, it must have looked to her like a strange new planet. There was no grass or sunshine here, just a large cold and sterile structure with elevators that moved from floor to floor, many levels of stairs to climb, long endless corridors with shiny linoleum floors, caustic smells, and closed doors. There were people scurrying down corridors and, in contrast, patients attached to IVs struggling with walkers while slowly making their way down the hallway. There were the gurneys being rushed urgently through the corridors on "stat" calls, and the pungent smells of illness that the canine nose recognizes. Therapy dogs must be trained to adapt to the hospital environment, with its sights and sounds and smells and sometimes chaos before they can begin working with patients.

We rode only the freight elevators so patients who might be frightened at the sight of a large dog, or who had compromised immune systems or allergies, would be protected. Often we walked three or four flights of stairs when the freight elevator was not available. It was a brand new experience for this young dog, and for me as well. I learned to locate the closets with the clean sheets for Holly to lie on, and how to carry a few at a time neatly folded over my arm while a Polaroid camera hung around my neck. Holly's lead encircled my left wrist as I guided her through the corridors, hugging the walls to be out of the way of staff and patients. It was a bit of a juggling act but the rewards we would receive made it well worth the trouble. No work would be more fulfilling than watching long sad faces change to broad smiles of joy the instant Holly appeared in the doorway of each room.

Before they could touch the dog, each patient would be asked to clean their hands with the Isogel cleanser which I carried in the pocket of my blue volunteer jacket. Hospitals are very diligent about not spreading infection through petting an animal, so this was a requirement.

On the second orientation, Holly made her first visit. As we stood in the doorway of his room, I watched Kc, an experienced nurse, cheerfully greet Mr. Johnson, a heart patient, in preparation for the visit he had requested. After a polite pause, Holly and I entered. The rule was: You don't barge right in with a dog. You are respectful of the person's privacy and needs. I kept Holly close to my side while making our introductions. The young man had undergone a heart transplant and his bare chest was decorated with electrodes to monitor his heart rhythm. He looked down at Holly, who was now wagging her excited tail, completely ignoring the wires, as well as his full beard and mustache, the first human with a beard she'd ever seen. Young dogs sometimes are nervous when exposed to something new. Once at a dog show, a young Golden Retriever took one look at me and backed away, barking fearfully. I was wearing a large hat. His handler handed me a cookie to give him to disarm the situation. And so he learned that people in hats were safe. But Holly seemed to adapt to these strange-looking people attached to machines without any need for cookies. And the beard was part of the experience.

"Mr. Johnson, would you like to have the dog on your bed?" I asked.

"Definitely," he responded, sliding over to make room for her. I spread one of the clean sheets over his blankets to serve as a barrier to dog hair. There were rules to follow. I lifted Holly's front paws onto the bedding, gave her rump a boost and she was up. I signaled her where to position herself by tapping my hand on the space next to the patient. She was to lie on the sheet, not on the man, respecting the wires and connections. The instant she was next to him, he reached out to touch her head. She seemed to be aware of the constraints of this small bed and didn't roll over on him. She lay by his side, not moving. He petted her with both hands, caressing her head and wherever else he could reach without disconnecting himself. After gazing into his eyes for a moment, Holly laid her chin on his arm and closed her eyes, melting into a state of total trust and relaxation. The cardiac patient closed his eyes and they lay in the bed together like old friends.

In the beginning, Holly watched me carefully for direction, turning her head toward me to ask with her inquisitive face if she was doing it right. She seemed to know she was working, and took it very seriously. For a dog not even a year old, she appeared mature and sensible, no hi-jinx, no silliness, no jumping around. She showed none of the behaviors she might have shown at home on *my* bed. She was obedient and respectful in the hospital. She looked for and waited for my words of approval. "Good girl," I told her.

At this point she was the only therapy dog in the program. There was no danger of her revealing our terrible secret, no danger of any aggression. Not yet.

Because I took a photo using the Polaroid camera, the patient could immediately receive a picture annotated with his name and Holly's and the date. He would remember the visit, share the photo with visitors and have something to talk about other than his illness. The picture showed Holly lying perfectly still on the hospital bed close to her new friend, while he held her tenderly with one hand on her head and the other on her back. The connection was beyond language. He would later ask that the poignant scene be tacked on the wall near his bed. These were intimate memories available any time he needed them.

Every working dog needs a time-out space. Kc showed us a secluded office where I could take Holly if she got tired or overstimulated. Normally dogs exercise, and then sleep. The therapy dog has to stay "on" for long periods of time, attentive to her patients, interacting with them, as well as the staff and visitors, with no rest period. I put out a water bowl and soft pad on the floor in a dark corner, a place to escape to, if things got chaotic, or if there was an emergency or too much clamor. But Holly took to people as naturally as she did to retrieving. She greeted the nurses, the doctors, the entire staff, and visitors with as much enthusiasm as she showed her patients; with her tail wagging and that irresistible eye contact, she let them know she was glad to see them. No one was exempt from her charm. Her popularity and reputation spread until her picture was displayed on hospital bulletin boards, and she was featured in the *L.A. Times* in her red Santa Claus hat and matching scarf with the headline: The dog-tor is in. The nurses called her Dr. Holly. It sounded great. But I secretly lived in fear of the day she would encounter another dog in the hospital and turn loose the demon dog who would ruin all of this. And that day was coming.

Keppel

"Ruth, you have a special visitor." The patient was propped up in a wheelchair with pillows under her head and appeared to be sleeping. Sarah, the Occupational Therapist tried to rouse her, but Ruth didn't open her eyes or respond to the gentle nudge on her arm.

Holly and I stood in the doorway of a private hospital room in Neuro-Psychiatrics. We were there in response to a request by the woman's family for a dog visit. But there was no movement or response from this patient. In most cases, the patients requested the pet visit and greeted us warmly with broad smiles. Some said they'd been waiting all day to meet Holly. This was different.

Sarah tried again. "Ruth, there's a beautiful Golden Retriever here to visit you." Still no movement in the chair. I waited in the doorway with Holly standing at my side and wondered how in the world my dog could make a connection with a non-responsive person.

Ruth's eyes did not open, and she seemed unaware that we were there. I was told by the psychiatric nurse that she was *catatonic*, a mental disorder involving immobility and rigidity. She had remained in the same position for several days, not moving or speaking. She was fed through a tube.

Three family members—two women and a man—were gathered around the frozen patient. The two women spoke what sounded like Yiddish. I was surprised to notice that Ruth was young, probably in her thirties. I had expected to see an older woman in this condition, although it was not an age-related disorder. Someone had dressed her and combed her long dark hair, pulling it back on each side with barrettes. She used to be pretty, I thought. Her face showed no expression now, and she looked as if she had died. How can we do anything? I thought. Neither Holly nor I had the skills to awaken the dead.

The nurse motioned for us to enter the room, and Holly moved immediately to greet the adults standing around as if they were the recipients of this visit. The family petted and fussed over her as I worried about what to do next. I told them that Holly was *a zeis kindt*, a sweet child. "zeis kindt". My mother called me zeis kindt when I was very little, and when she liked me. I knew three or four Yiddish words, and these were two of them.

The other word I knew was *keppel,* an affectionate form of *kop*, meaning head. My mother sometimes said I had *a keppala*, a nice little head. I had once taught Holly keppel as an invitation to put her head in my lap. I would point to my lap and say keppel and she would lay her head there.

Out of desperation, and not knowing how else to make this happen, I said "Holly, keppel," while I lightly tapped the woman's knees with my hand.

My dog approached the lifeless woman and put her golden head on the still lap. The family was impressed that Holly understood Yiddish. But there was no response from the woman in the chair. Holly stayed with her, not moving, waiting to be acknowledged. She seemed to know someone was in that shell of a body. She would simply wait, as she had learned to do with the

Alzheimer patients, wait...as she had learned to do when she wanted me to open doors for her. She knew how to wait.

We all saw it. Ruth slowly moved her hands to touch what she felt in her lap. With her eyes closed, she reached out to explore Holly's head, as her astonished family looked on. With both of her hands, she ran her fingertips over the dog's face. She felt the eyelids, and eyelashes, then the high forehead and the smooth top of the oval head. Holly sat still, not moving or flinching, just allowing herself to be felt and known.

Everyone in the room seemed to stop breathing and stood in silence. The inquisitive hands slid down to caress the velvety ears and the thick furry neck. The movements were those of a blind person seeing with her hands. The family took a needed breath and gasped aloud, almost in unison. I looked at Sarah across the room. She was starting to tear up.

Holly moved away when the petting stopped. I led her back so she could do it again. I repeated, "Keppel," and she knew what to do. The quiet hand reached down once again and stroked the head lying on her legs. The family members sighed, and spoke Yiddish to each other. I heard the word, "Keppel."

The catatonic patient never spoke or opened her eyes. But she clearly felt the dog's presence. The therapist explained that this was the first time the woman had responded to anyone since she'd been there. She was moving, touching, and interacting with the dog. There was life! When we left the room, each member of the family thanked me with tears in their eyes, and caressed Holly's face, calling her *seis hindt* (sweet dog). The older woman, probably the mother, kissed my hands. I was crying too. These are the moments. Animals can be the source of our connection to each other. The healing energy in that room affected every one of us.

Holly and I returned to the Day Room where I sat on the sofa with my dog lying at my feet while I wrote my commentary in the

PAC log. Sarah and I reviewed what had just happened. She was still in shock.

One week later, when we were in the unit for our weekly visit, I asked about Ruth.

"Oh, she went home a few days ago," Sarah told me. "She's okay now."

I guess I used the right word.

My Worst Nightmare

AT SIX PM THURSDAY night, I answered the phone and was surprised to hear Kc's voice. As director of the People-Animal Connection Program at UCLA, she usually called to discuss the PAC evaluations we did together, and get my opinion on which of the teams tested should pass or fail. Sometimes we talked for hours and it was difficult to stop. But we had just completed those last month. I wondered what prompted this evening's call. Holly and I were to be at the hospital the next day, our scheduled Friday. I was just getting ready to bathe her for that visit. I looked at the clock and wondered if my evening was gone.

"Would you like to be interviewed tomorrow by Candice Bergen for the *Today Show*?" she asked. I took a deep breath and felt my stomach drop to my feet. I didn't answer. She went on "She's doing a piece about the PAC program at UCLA and will be filming here all day Friday. I thought since you're an integral part of our program, you should be included in this piece." I felt weak. Be on television? Me? My hands were clammy holding the phone.

All I could say was "I don't think so."

"But you're so good and bring so much to the patients," she argued. "Can't they film Holly and me doing our session in 2 South? We're there tomorrow anyway." I would be willing to be filmed working with my dog. I knew we were good as a team. But an interview on camera where I had to sound brilliant without leaning on Holly's brilliance as a therapist? Too scary.

"No cameras are allowed in NPH," she said. I knew this because whenever there was media coverage, we were not included. The film crews were not invited into Neuro-Psychiatrics, and my work with Holly was never videotaped. If you were a cardiac patient, camera crews were invited at patient discretion. That was not a secretive disorder, but psychiatric units still carried the stigma of the old "lunatic" asylums.

"Couldn't we get written permission from the parents of the adolescents in 2 South?" I asked.

"No, they won't let us film in there. It's a rule," Kc answered. It sounded final.

"I don't want to describe the sessions we do. I want to show them."

"Sorry—it won't happen" she said. "You can be interviewed by Candice Bergen but no way will they allow cameras into NPH."

"I'm too uncomfortable with that" I told her. What I didn't say was that I trusted Holly and the strategies we used as long as we were safely behind closed doors. But an interview somewhere else? What if Holly aggressed toward another dog? And what would I say? How would I describe what I do? I had given talks about Animal-Assisted Therapy. But an interview on camera? I couldn't prepare for that. I didn't know what would be asked. I shrank from the offer to be interviewed for T.V. like the coward I knew I was.

"Kc, I'm just too nervous talking about the work and not doing it."

"Okay," she said. "But you were asked. I couldn't leave you out."

"Thanks for thinking of me." I hung up feeling saddened. I

ached for recognition. Yet when it was offered, I was afraid I'd say the wrong thing, or stumble over a word. Worst of all, I couldn't trust my dog to behave if other dogs were in the vicinity. What if she growled? Therapy dogs don't do that. They can't do that. What if in the middle of the television interview, Holly showed her menacing grimace toward another dog? I would be humiliated. I didn't trust her. I also didn't trust myself to do it right. The legacy of my life continued.

    I lay awake all night in conflict about this. The following day Holly was groomed and ready to go to work. I felt tense as we carefully made our way through hospital corridors avoiding the bustle of camera crews. They could be seen entering cardio care, intensive care, pediatrics, orthopedics, everywhere except the psychiatric units. We took the freight elevator directly to the 2nd floor to 2 South, Adolescent Psychiatry, our home base where I felt safe and competent. We did our usual successful session with the teenage population. I felt disappointed that the cameras were not allowed in there. Then the world would know how good we were. We were applauded by the staff before we left. Holly was always a hit. Afterward, I felt shaky again because I knew what was taking place all around the hospital. I wanted to go home. But part of me longed to be acknowledged for the work I did.

    We went down to the lobby and made our way to the patio outside the Volunteer office. In the distance I noticed a small crowd of people and a few dogs out on the grassy plaza level surrounded by cameramen, tripods, with the natural lighting of the sun. In the center of the circle, the star and interviewer, Candice Bergen, blonde and still stunning in a navy blue blazer and slacks, sat on a stone wall holding a mic to someone's face, talking to some of the volunteers who sat in a circle around her with their beautifully behaved dogs sitting quietly at their sides.

    When I don't know what to do, I do nothing. I sat on a

bench on the patio to wait till they were gone. I ached to be included. I was an important part of the program, just as Kc had said. I didn't feel good about being left out. Maybe we could do this. I looked down at Holly as she lay politely at my feet. Do you think we could go over there and join them on camera? I wondered. Could I risk that this therapy dog who had just been impeccable in her work in NPH would embarrass, or humiliate me. Could I trust her? Could I trust myself? I felt ashamed that I was frightened. I did nothing, just sat in the sun wearing dark sunglasses and waiting to figure it out.

The double glass doors to the hospital swung open and a young woman wearing a blue volunteer jacket strolled toward us with her teammate, a shiny black Lab wearing the unmistakeable blue and gold PAC scarf around his neck. I'd never seen either of them before. Neither had Holly. As if a fire alarm had gone off in her head, my 'therapy' dog jumped to her feet. I hung onto the lead tightly in my hand. We were still attached, thank god. Without waiting to find out who they were, or checking out the dog, she charged toward them, baring her teeth and barking in a loud shrill tone, like a war-cry. She was warning, "Go away, or I will attack you."

It was an eerie sound in a hospital where barking dogs were never heard. I gripped the lead as it cut into my hand. She tried to pull away from me, rising up on her hind legs and pawing the air in a fierce effort to get free, while continuing her high-pitched, shrieking calls of alarm. With all my strength I yanked her back, yelling, "No." Holly was in full-blown aggression. On a scale of one to ten, she had gone straight to ten; this was the dreaded "red zone." The stunned girl held onto her Lab, her mouth opened as if to protest this unprovoked threatening and wild maniac dog in attack mode. Wearing her UCLA PAC scarf, Holly looked as inappropriate as a Marine in combat wearing a beanie cap. The volunteer dragged her confused dog away and fled the scene as I called out pitifully, "I'm sorry." It was clear we were both PAC volunteers. There was no mistaking our uniforms. She and I had never met, which meant she was new to the program. It was clear both of our canines were therapy dogs working in the hospital. Damn. She would surely report this incident to the director, Kc.

We were undone, exposed. My dark dirty secret was out. We'd be asked to leave the program. My life would be over. A PAC dog can NEVER aggress. In the behavioral evaluations, it was an automatic FAIL. As a Delta evaluator, I certainly knew this was not acceptable. I had failed teams for a lot less than aggression. It was unthinkable. Holly and I were the most experienced team; the first PAC team in the hospital. I was a consultant and trainer for new teams to NPH, a speaker and Animal-Assisted Therapy specialist. Holly was the "demo" dog for PAC. Volunteers were sent in to observe her sessions and learn. She was supposed to be perfect. This was a nightmare. I felt sick to my stomach. We were being revealed as frauds.

I wanted to run away, hide, get to my car, get out of there, lick my wounded pride, cry. I grabbed Holly's lead. She was still frothing with leftover aggression. I had to walk around the plaza level to get to the elevator to the lower parking level and to my car. We passed the group of PAC teams being interviewed and filmed. I marched her as quickly as I could along the path around the grassy square. When we were nearly at the elevators, Betty, one of the volunteers, called my name and motioned for me to come over and get in on the filming. She was with Kolya, her Great White Pyrenees, a gorgeous dog, the "gentle giant" they are known to be. I waved hello, but shook my head negatively to the offer, and motioned toward my dog. Betty walked closer to us and said, "You should be in this." I had to tell her. "She's been naughty. We're going home." I felt this was an understatement. She had been more than "naughty." She had tried to murder someone—not the innocent Labrador—ME. In revealing these monstrous behaviors to the world, all my good work was erased. A lifetime of efforting to be successful had been killed. I had failed.

Abruptly, Holly, who was still apparently in the "red" zone, tried to go after Kolya, barking loudly, leaping up and pulling toward her. I hung onto her ferociously. Kolya was a dog she knew, the most passive of all the dogs in the program. This shouldn't be happening. I couldn't get away fast enough. I was on the edge of tears and Betty saw it. We made it to the car. I put Holly in the back seat saying nothing to her. I wanted to say, "You are a disgrace, you let me down, you're a bad dog." I really wanted to say that my mother was right. I was a bad child.

My hands shook as I turned the key in the ignition. There were tears in my eyes. I had failed in public. It wasn't a secret anymore. Everyone knew. I never got anything right.

I WAS FIVE YEARS old in kindergarten, wanting to cry because I couldn't paste the pieces of cut-out construction paper into the shape of the Easter bunny. I knew even then that I was incompetent. I was nineteen and lying in the snow with skis askew, holding back the tears because I couldn't get up and I was cold. The more I tried to lift myself with my arms, the weaker I felt. All I could think about were my father's words when I asked to go skiing. He warned me firmly. "You can't ski, you'll fall down, you'll freeze to death." He was right. I was defective.

For the next few nights I was an insomniac staring at the green neon light from the radio clock next to my bed, worrying and dreading the inevitable phone call. I imagined that Kc would call me and apologetically explain that this kind of incident could shut down the PAC program which accepted only well-behaved dogs that could be trusted with patients at all times. She would say, "I'm so sorry. You and Holly have been a remarkable team and have helped so many patients in the hospital and in NPI. But you know the rules. We cannot allow any dog in our program who displays aggression." I would say "I know. I understand. I'm so sorry." And I would feel humiliated.

Holly would never have been accepted into the program if she had shown her dark side during the behavioral evaluation every potential therapy dog must pass. She was tested seven years earlier and was the first dog to be certified. The only dog she had to meet was Kiley, Kc's Golden. Holly and Kiley had already met for a beach date, so by the time of the evaluation, Kiley was no longer a threat. She was no longer the "neutral" dog in the evaluation; a dog Holly should never have met before. I guess we had cheated. But now the secret I had so carefully guarded was out. Kc would be sincerely sad about missing us. But we would be out of the program. She would have no choice. And that would be the end of my career as an Animal-Assisted Therapy Specialist, as a consultant and trainer for the new teams, and. as the handler of a great therapy dog. How in the world could I have a dog with problems when I was there to solve problems and improve the program's services to patients? Another failure on my list.

This reminded me of being questioned about how I could be a Marriage and Family therapist when I myself was divorced. Someone said, "How can you help couples when you failed marriage?" I remember saying, "Well, you don't have to be a prima ballerina to teach ballet." I thought that was a good answer.

The dreaded phone call never came. Apparently the incident was not reported to the director. I can only imagine that the new volunteer was worried about being in an undesignated area and somehow felt fearful that she would be reprimanded. She never called it in. Once again we were saved from impending disgrace.

Water Dog

When I was six years old, my father tried to drown me in the Atlantic Ocean. He picked me up in his arms at Brighton Beach, walked into the water waist-deep and threw me out into the ocean, shouting, "Swim!"

I didn't know how to swim. The waves rolled over me as I went under. Unable to breath, I felt the desperate panic of gasping for air and swallowing water. "So this is what drowning is," I thought. Finally, his hands appeared again and scooped me up, I coughing and sputtering salt water. I didn't get into water for another thirty years, even keeping my face out of the shower spray. He had said that it was time for me to learn how to swim. This was the way he learned.

He fell, or was pushed, into the East River in New York City. He was also six years old. He would have drowned if not for his dog Spot, who jumped in with him and paddled next to him, encouraging him to stay afloat. My father struggled to keep up with the swimming dog and followed him to shore. Sink or swim, he always said. My father was born at the turn of the century on the East Side of Manhattan, became a gang kid, and a survivor. He thought I should get over my fear of deep water by being thrown headlong right into it. Sink or swim, just as he had. I sank. I didn't have a dog to save me.

Golden Retrievers are natural swimmers. They don't have to be taught. Just offer them deep water and they will swim. When Holly was eight months old, I decided it was time for her to have this fulfilling experience. I took her to the beach in Malibu and tossed her obsession, the yellow tennis ball, into the ocean. She happily chased after it as she did on grass, cement, or on dirt trails. She ran right into the surf, but when the rush of turbulent waves rose up in her path, she turned away from the roar and thunder of this unknown predator and ran back to the beach without the prize in her mouth. When the tide receded, she thought it was safe to try again, but the next swell had gathered its force and once again she retreated to the beach. Back and forth she ran all afternoon as if the tides were chasing her, frothing at her heels. I watched her come running toward me that day on the beach, with the waves crashing behind her, carrying nothing in her mouth. Each time the tide lost its fury and was sucked back into the sea, she turned to face the enemy, as if she had won the battle and vanquished the attacker. She would venture back into the safety of shallow, still, waters determined to find that floating elusive prey. I kept throwing new ones, an instant cue to evoke prey drive in any retriever, and she'd chase after them until the next breaker started to build. Then she'd submit respectfully to its power and retreat once again. The balls were carried back to shore by the tide, and in the benign shallow water, she'd scoop them up in her mouth, one at a time, and bring them to me triumphantly. But she had not conquered this ocean yet. She was running, not swimming.

One day I took her to a small lagoon where there was no surf, and threw her ball. She chased after it, running into the still water until she reached the spot where she could no longer touch bottom. She turned back to look at me for direction, her brows furrowed, mouth closed, and her ears cocked. I yelled, "Go get it, Holly." There was no roar, or threat of high tides to deter her this time. She turned away from me, her eyes on the floating ball, and let go of the safety of the muddy floor beneath her feet. She let her retriever instinct take over, and those wonderful legs born to swim became paddles and cycled her through the calm water. She was swimming for the first time in her life.

She seized that tennis ball, turned and swam back to me holding it in her open mouth and offered it to me, tail wagging wildly, as happy and accomplished as someone who just completed swimming the English Channel. She shook herself off and looked at my face for a response to this amazing feat. Her mouth was curved in that retriever smile, her eyes bright, her tail wagging with pride as if to say, "Did you see what I can do? Did you see me swim?"

My joy matched hers. "Good girl," I told her. But she knew. Swimming to retrieve prey was in her DNA makeup.

Now it was time to go back to her nemesis, the ocean, and face her fear of moving water and crashing waves. It was a sunny clear day, but the tides were high and noisy in their descent. I threw the ball out as far as I could. Holly bounded into the surf after it, dove right under the whitecapped waves, and disappeared. I heard the thunderous water explode over my last glimpse of her, and looked out over the vast expanse of ocean, gulls flying overhead, blue sky, open sea. There was no sign of my dog. She had been sucked up by the ocean. Had I sent her down to the bottom of the sea to drown? I held my breath. I was going down. I felt the water closing in over me. I couldn't breathe. I was drowning.

I prayed she'd be there when the wave completed its ride to the beach. I prayed I wasn't being punished. I prayed I had not become my father.

"Dear god, where is she?" Suddenly a scraggly wet golden head bobbed up, holding something in her open mouth. This dog bred to retrieve ducks shot out of the sky by hunters, bred to swim out and bring them in unscathed in a soft mouth, bred to be a fearless and confident swimmer, had just earned the title "retriever."

And in that instant she was no longer a scared puppy; she was doing the work she had to do to fulfill her life. And I had faced my worst fears right along with her. My catastrophic fear of losing someone I loved, and my fear of drowning were both re-enacted through Holly's ultimate triumph.

My first attempts at swimming were while wearing the "Esther Williams" smile, head above water, face and hair dry. Although I was never to be an ocean swimmer, years later I joined a national organization called the U.S. Masters Swimming and with professional coaching became an accomplished swimmer. I learned to put my face underwater, slowly exhaling each breath, and then turning my head to the side for the life-giving breaths of air, as I propelled my strong arms and legs through the cool water. Holly and I had both conquered our fear of water. We had not drowned. We were still here. And we were swimmers.

Holly couldn't get enough of the water game. Playing on the beach and chasing the surf to retrieve her ball were the most joyous times of her life, and watching her lifted me out of the childhood depression of my life into what must be called happiness.

EIGHT YEARS LATER, I was handed what felt like my death sentence. Holly had cancer. My friend Nina helped me survive. "Now is the time to give her everything she loves. Let her dig for gophers, chase the squirrels, take her to the beach, and let her swim and retrieve her beloved tennis ball in the ocean."

And that's what we did. With three dogs crammed into the car, we drove up the coast past Malibu to a dog beach. Holly and her best friend Mikimoto, a West-Highland-White-Terrier, had grown up together, wrestling and playing since they were four-month-old puppies in the park. Holly became a full sized retriever, while Miki stayed the little Westie terrier, always allowed to climb all over this adult sixty-five pound Golden Retriever, sitting on her, lying on top of her, walking across her with total permission from the larger dog. The youngest Westie was Bunny, still a puppy herself. They were jolly on the beach together, while Auntie Nina filmed all of it. With her digital camera she recorded for me Holly's last beach day. My dog came loping along with a slight limp in her rear left leg from arthritis, flinging sand, burying her tennis ball, then digging it up again, placing the muddy thing right in my hand to throw, and chasing after it until she couldn't walk anymore. Even then she hobbled after her ball, holding one leg up and running on the other three, then swimming as if she had no arthritis. Again, and again she'd carry the ball back to me, and drop it from her soft mouth into my open hand, her eyes looking into mine, watching my face for approval.

Yes, you are my water dog.

I GO TO THE beach alone now. Dogs dig holes in the sand, run in and out of the surf, tails wagging in sheer joy, and I smile and live a thousand lifetimes with Holly all over again.

Letting Go

HOLLY LOOKED DOWN INTO the swimming pool, paws extended over the edge, intently watching as her ball on a rope floated away. Her head and shoulders thrust forward, wanting desperately to retrieve it, but not at the risk of leaping into the air with an uncertain landing. The adolescents of 2 South called, "Holly, get it." She had strong prey drive, and would chase anything moving: a leaf, a ball, a bird, a squirrel (her favorite) or my slipper tossed across the room. Her body rocked precariously on the ledge as if she was about to let go and take the plunge. But then she backed up, and looked at me with that helpless stare.

It was summer now; the days were warm, and the outdoor swimming pool of the Psychiatric Hospital was open. Gail, the Recreational Therapist invited me to conduct animal-assisted therapy sessions at the pool instead of in the hospital. I accepted these invitations gladly. After all, I had more than just a therapy dog. She was a retriever; bred to leap into ice cold streams or lakes, mouth the bird shot out of the sky without injuring a single feather, swim to the shore and carry it to her companion, the hunter, presenting an unscathed bird. I had a water dog.

With a swim-suit underneath my slacks and UCLA blue jacket, I came fully prepared to get wet along with Holly. Gail met us on the pool deck looking like a life guard with a whistle around her neck. The kids were already splashing around, some playing volley-ball with a freedom of movement they didn't show inside the walls of the hospital. The water seemed to calm and soothe them.

When I unhooked Holly's collar with its jangling tags, and untied her UCLA blue and gold scarf, her behavior also changed. She was no longer the calm therapy dog who worked in adolescent psychiatry. She became excited and ran her joyous 'victory laps' all around the pool perimeter. Removing her 'uniform' signaled that she was 'off duty,' and no longer a working dog. The sight and sounds of water added to her frenzy and I had to hold onto her neck with both hands to restrain her.

The PAC director, Kc, always concerned about safety issues, warned that the kids couldn't be in the water at the same time as the dog. She recalled nearly drowning when a swimming dog accidentally placed a paw on her shoulder, pulling her underwater. I assumed hospital insurance would not cover a drowning during a group therapy session and made the disappointing announcement. The kids groaned and booed. "I want to swim with Holly" yelled Jason, a ten-year-old with attention-deficit disorder and hyperactivity, as he circled the pool in loud protest. I had to be as creative as possible to make the session work.

I asked the teen-agers to wait on the steps of the pool for their turn to throw a ball attached to a rope as far as they could into the water. Holly was to swim out and retrieve it, hold it in her mouth, then swim back and return it to the thrower. The first ball was tossed out by Eddie, a wiry eleven-year-old, so nervous about being first, he dropped the rope behind him twice before he finally figured out how to swing it in the air and hurl it forward. The ball landed at the deep end of the pool. Good throw! Holly never took her eyes off it. I released her and gave her the signal, "Holly get it."

The retriever raced down the steps, pushing off the last one, and treading smoothly through the pool's blue water until she reached the floating ball. She mouthed the rope attached to it, and with the ball dangling, turned back toward Eddie, holding onto her prey without so much as a splash.

"Look at her feet, she swims like a duck" he called, watching her glide through the water. Reaching the steps, she dropped the ball into his waiting hand. Everyone applauded. Eddie smiled proudly at his accomplishment. Most of the kids had never seen a retriever's feet padding through water with the ease and grace of an amphibian with webbed toes. "She was born to swim" I said. But not in a pool!

At the beach, Holly would race from the sand into the surf, chasing her yellow tennis ball, and when her feet could no longer touch the ocean floor, she would propel those athletic legs through the water like paddles, undaunted by the turbulent tides, disappearing under a crashing wave, but never losing track of her prize. She would reach for it with her mouth, turn and swim back to me, drop it into my hand, and then stand in the shallow water, poised for the next throw.

In a pool, she had to learn to use the concrete steps to get out. She would swim in circles, getting tired as she searched for the non-existing shoreline. The kids sat on the steps calling "Holly, here" and she soon discovered which way was out.

But the one activity that still eluded her was jumping off the ledge of the pool, a drop of several feet into the water. She would stand there staring at the ball drifting away, while we all yelled in chorus, "Holly jump." Her head turned toward me, and her eyes asked for help with this dilemma. Holly looked at me for everything she wanted. I was the keeper of her ball, toys, food and water, her walks, her comfort or discomfort, her freedom or confinement. As a pack leader, I was responsible for her survival.

If she hurt her paw, she would hold it up and look at me pathetically. It was not surprising that as the bobbing ball moved further away from her, she stared hard at me. But this time I did not help her. She would have to jump into the pool and retrieve it for herself. She had to face her fears just like the rest of us.

IN ADOLESCENT PSYCHIATRY, FEAR was a powerful motivator. Angry and defiant at twelve years old, Patty usually sauntered into the group sessions ready for battle, her fists clenched and legs poised to kick anyone in her way. She would be removed within minutes of her tirade, fighting and swearing at the staff as she was taken back to her room. She was never present long enough to interact with Holly Go Lightly, the canine therapist. Typically, Patty stayed hidden away avoiding all social contact.

But in the swimming pool, Patty took on a different demeanor. Floating on her back, isolated from the group, she appeared peaceful without the 'oppositional-defiance' that described her behaviors in clinical reports that stated she would stand when told to sit and throw her books on the floor when asked to open one. The water was therapeutic for her. There was freedom here. She didn't show the aggression that had landed her in a psychiatric residential setting. She had been expelled from public school and labeled a 'conduct disorder' because she fought with everyone and incited large brawls on the school playground. In class and in therapy she refused to follow rules and procedures, walking out, and spewing obscenities at her teachers and therapists alike.

While Holly stood at the edge of the pool testing her confidence, I seized the opportunity to talk with the group about being afraid. They knew about fear; Patty especially. I learned that she had suffered physical abuse from the man her mother lived with. Patty's mother was unable to control her behavior and described her simply as a "bad kid." Protective services finally removed her from the home, and since she was out of control, referred her for psychiatric evaluation and treatment. With nowhere to go and little change in her behavior, she was still in residence at the hospital.

I didn't ask them to talk about what made them afraid. My technique was always to use Holly as the facilitator; keeping the focus on the child's relationship with the dog.

"How can we help Holly to overcome her fear of jumping into the pool?' I asked. Several children spoke up. Alan, a 15-year-old said, "Throw her in....she'll get over it." An older girl, Barbara, about 17, said, "No, just pet her and be kind to her, and she'll act brave." Unknowingly, they were talking about how they dealt with their own demons. Alan showed bravado, suppressing any doubts or anxieties he might feel. It was difficult to relate to him, so protective was his cover. Barbara was withdrawn. She needed special attention before she would engage in most activities. She did little on her own without someone to encourage her.

Patty spoke for herself.

"Well, we need to show her that it's safe." This was an answer made in heaven, and coming from this child, it was profound. I jumped at the chance to use it.

"How can we show her it's safe?" I asked.

"She can watch me," she explained, and in that instant, the young girl stood next to Holly at the edge of the pool and leaped into the air as if on a diving board, coming down feet first, straight into the water, splashing everyone around her. Now she began paddling about, watching the dog's reaction. Holly just stared. One at a time, the other kids followed Patty's lead, showing the dog how it was done, until the entire group of nine children had landed in the pool splashing and thrashing around in the water. Some of them swam back and forth in front of Holly calling her name. The retriever inched forward, her paws hanging over the edge, yet still—she hesitated.

They began calling in unison, "Holly jump. Holly jump." Patty grabbed the roped ball, threw it across the pool and swam after it, modeling for Holly what she was supposed to do, while the kids continued chanting, "Holly jump." She leaned over and stared straight down as if she was measuring the height of the drop into the water. She was almost in. Still they coaxed her. It had become a group project, and it was thrilling to see these children, usually isolated and depressed, now smiling and calling and encouraging this hesitant and fearful dog to take the risk and to let go. They were working together as a group. The therapist was speechless. She grabbed my hand, squeezing it. Not only was Patty part of the group effort, she was leading it. Socialization was the primary goal for these teenagers, and they were achieving it.

Finally Holly could wait no longer. She let go of the safety of her concrete perch, and like a bird leaving the nest, dove into the air and hit the water with a resounding splash. She sailed after her ball as if it was alive. The kids cheered. The staff cheered. Even the pool manager cheered. Holly captured the prey, the object of her courage, scooped it up with her mouth, and headed toward the steps of the pool, where Patty sat waiting for her. Holly released the ball from her mouth to Patty's hand, following the protocol of retrieving to the thrower. In those few moments, this child had become the leader of the pack. Holly's mouth parted to reveal the famous golden grin as if she knew she had fulfilled her legacy as a retriever. She had conquered her fear of leaping from a high ground into a body of water, a skill that all working retrievers must have. I underlined this occasion.

"You taught her not to be afraid." I called out to the group. Every child smiled with pride.

And then I looked at Patty, sitting on the steps, with hair

soaked and glowing sun-burned face. Her arms were wrapped tightly around the neck of the wet dog, her face nuzzled against Holly's. I said directly to her.

"And *you* showed her *how* to do it,—just let go and trust the water."

"Yes," she smiled, "I showed her it was safe." Patty turned and kissed the top of Holly's head, right on the oval bump that I always call the "smart bump.' The kids splashed their way over to this pair, and proceeded to pet and hug the dog, telling her how brave she had been. There was lots of chatter, and laughter and celebration. We would all remember this day. The kids from 2 South had become empowered by this simple act of bravery by an animal, paired with the cooperative effort of the group. The water was a metaphor for facing their fears. In helping Holly let go and jump, perhaps they would find their own courage.

After that day, the therapy dog was willing to jump into the pool without all the hullabaloo. Just the throw of her beloved tennis ball and the words, "Holly jump" and she would leap into the water with confidence. Patty left her room to come to all of our therapy sessions in the hospital or at the pool, to check on Holly. She needed to make sure that *Holly* was not nervous or afraid anymore.

Alone Again

She saw them before I did. They were running down the street toward us, a man and his dog. Holly froze, locked her jaw, narrowed her eyes, projected her head forward and emitted a deep growl. She was an animal ready to attack. My jaw locked as well, and I could feel my breath became shallow and rapid; I tightened the lead in my hand. This was not supposed to happen. She had been rehabilitated by my friend Nina, a tough disciplinarian and dog trainer. She would never aggress toward new dogs again. I had seen her progress with my own eyes. Holly was calm and stable around strange dogs when Nina was in charge. It was apparent that I was not to be trusted as leader of this pack of two.

Holly would not budge from the spot. I hung onto her tightly, the leather lead cutting into my hand. The man was jogging along, unaware that his approach was being measured and prepared for by this defensive canine. At his side, a large white Lab only needed to walk briskly to keep up with him. Neither man nor dog looked concerned or noticed the build up of physical tension.

When they had crossed the imaginary safety line and were entering her space, Holly reared up on her hind legs and thrashed the air, upper lip flattened against her mouth, her teeth bared. She let out a snarling battle cry, a long drooling whine followed by shrieking barks. The man and his dog jogged past us, with barely a glance, as I struggled to hold onto her with both hands pulling back on the lead. I was nearly pulled off my feet.

Nina had taught me to deal with her aggression by grabbing her by the neck and throwing her over, pinning her to the ground. I grabbed her and with all my strength, tried to throw her over. She wouldn't go down. I kept trying to shove her onto her side. She had to submit to me. I dug my fingers into her thick fur. She snarled and reared up, then I watched her turn her head and eyes in my direction, and slowly and deliberately she gazed directly at me. I realized that the target was no longer the jogging Lab who had long since disappeared around the block. It was me. I was the enemy. She lunged at my hands that were trying to throw her over and punctured my skin, drawing blood. These were the same hands that petted, fed and cared for all of her needs. There was no loyalty, no gratitude, no compassion, certainly no love in this attack. This was not supposed to happen.

This wasn't a Pit Bull, she was a goddam Golden Retriever. I grabbed at her neck with my hands, kicking at her with my feet. Her response was to snarl and growl at me, and to bite down on both of my hands until I could see the blood streaking down my arms. I strung her with the kennel lead high up on her neck to cut off her air like a hangman's noose. I had practiced this with Nina's instruction as an alternative to pinning her on the ground. She gasped, and afraid that I would choke her to death, that I would kill this dog who was now attacking me, I released the noose. Mistake! I should have continued choking her. Not the time for pity. She certainly showed me no mercy.

She rolled back her lips to show me again those pointed canine teeth. I noted the warning. She was threatening to seriously injure me. I screamed, "No!" and hung her again. I was trying to act brave but was terrified. That was her advantage. I was afraid of her, and she knew it. I remembered the recurrent horror stories of being bitten by a large black dog. I remembered how many times my mother reminded me not to trust them, each time she dragged me by the arm to avoid dogs on the street, to the puppies continuously banned from refuge in the cellar, to the caged canaries, her final solution to the problem. I guess I was always afraid of this moment. We never escape our early training. My mother's fear of dogs had been with me all along. Now it was my fear.

Suspecting I might actually choke her to death, I released the tight noose around her neck. She took this as a sign of further weakness, and now enraged, she threw herself at me, snapping at my hands again. I was bleeding all over her. We were in battle. I acted fierce, but she smelled my terror, along with my blood. This was the same kind of fear I displayed fighting back with all my strength when "Crazy Tom," a 250-pound, six-foot-five profoundly disturbed alcoholic I was married to for eight turbulent months had attacked me. He covered my mouth and nose with his large strong hands, pressing down on my nose to try and break it.

"I'll smash that pretty face so no one will ever look at you again," he said. I struggled to pull his hands off my face and couldn't budge them. My mouth and nose were covered. I had no air. He kicked me in the groin with cowboy boots. This was what he really thought of women.

"I will kill you if you ever try to leave me," he whispered close to my face as he gripped it with his hands. My nose was bleeding, my genitals aching and bruised.

"I'm not afraid of you, I will fight you to the death" were the words I could not speak. I fought back as he punched me in the face and kicked me. This man who had said he loved me, who had taken me to a new level of erotic passion, was trying to kill me.

The rush of this adrenalin memory turned to fury and was

unleashed against this dog who had been the love of my life. I tried to pin her again, and she fought me, snarling and snapping at me. She grimaced as I hung her with the kennel lead, a tight noose around her neck until she gasped and I let go. Instead, I kicked at her, screaming, "No, you will not attack me!" This was for her, and for all those who had come before. "You will not attack me!" Now she fought to live. Her pupils pin pricks, her gaping mouth drooling with ugly snarling sounds, deep within her throat, warning, warning. She looked like a wolf.

I was losing. We were visible, on the grassy hill in front of the corner condo, overlooking the guard shack as cars drove past us entering the complex. No one stopped to help me, or to rescue her from what must have looked like animal abuse.

I took the tight noose around her neck and dragged her all the way home, threw her in the house, and immediately tried to pin her. She must submit to me. But she prepared to attack anew, her menacing stare and low growls aimed right at my face as she crouched in her dog bed in the downstairs entry way. This time I stopped, and pulled my bleeding hands away from her snarling mouth.

She had won.

The humiliation of kicking my dog in public and being stared at by the gardeners and lord only knows who else stung more deeply than the bleeding cuts on my hands and fingers. That I would ever kick or hit or try to hurt an animal is so completely heinous an act to me. That I could be driven so crazy is impossible for me to accept. Later I learned that I didn't kick hard enough or in the right place. I'm not a good dog fighter.

Why do I have to fight for my life? Why must I be battered by everyone, even my dog?

I was the little sister repeatedly beaten up at the hands of a brother I had adored, looked up to, and worshipped as my hero.

His hands that had stroked and comforted me when I was chased home by the school bullies now were hitting at me, and arms that had held me lovingly when I was scared now pushed me off my feet. There was no rescue in sight from my passive parents who had put him in charge of discipline.

YEARS LATER WHEN I was nearly twenty, this brother who was about to be married would abandon me, leaving me with them.

It was winter in Brooklyn. Rob and I were both invited to our cousin's engagement party. It was snowing and the temperature was dropping rapidly. I asked him if I could ride with him since we were both going to the same party. I was not allowed to drive yet. He drove my dad's car and said he couldn't take me because his soon-to-be wife wanted him to pick her up and go straight to the party on the other side of Brooklyn. For me this meant a train and two buses in the snow and cold and darkness of a New York night.

"If you let her boss you around now, what are you gonna do after you're married?" I hit him with that. I chose these words to hurt him with my sense of betrayal. He had chosen her. My brother, the athlete, always responding physically, having no skill with verbal defenses, smashed me in the face with his fist, my nose bloody, lip bleeding, skin soon to show purple bruises, as I hit the floor. He ran from the room and left the house.

I picked myself up, used ice packs, cleaned up the blood, and dressed warmly, determined to go to the party. I took the train and the buses and arrived quite late, making sure everyone saw my face and knew the cause of this injury. I wanted to shame him.

ALL OF THIS EXPLODED into my memory as I fought for my life with this dog I had also loved.

I tried so hard to take charge of all aspects of my existence, to become a confident leader of the pack, and instead was attacked in retaliation by my own sweet, loving therapy dog. Everyone loved Holly; she was the darling of the neighborhood. For Christ's sake, she was a therapy dog! She was supposed to be a healer. It was surreal. Someone would surely report me to animal regulation for dog abuse. Was it supposed to be so hard?

A friend once told me Holly was given to me to help heal my injuries. Now she was trying to kill me. I ran upstairs, and picked up the phone to call Nina. She would tell me what to do. I punched the numbers, misdialing. I tried again. My breathing was ragged. She answered. Thank god.

I told her what had just occurred. "What do I do right now? I dragged her home before she could even potty," I cried into the phone, looking at my ripped nails and the cuts on my hands. I listened to her calm response.

"Bring her to you? For two weeks?" I glanced around and spied Holly now lying on her dog bed, peacefully licking her paws. "Really?"

Nina said Holly had forgotten. She promised to coach me again. I was shaken, still bleeding, the phone was bloody. I needed to wash and put something on all this mess.

I trembled as I washed off the blood and covered the cuts with bandages. I raced around, packed up Holly's green comforter bed, her food, her vitamins, her glucosamine for arthritis, and then actually started counting out the number of cookies she'd need for two weeks.

Cookies? Was I nuts? This dog tried to put me in the hospital and I'm counting cookies. I dragged her to the car, threw her in the back seat, and drove to Nina's apartment. "Auntie Nina" was tough. She exuded dominant energy with her dogs, and they didn't dare misbehave. All she had to do was glare at them and they'd flop down on their bellies, showing pure submission.

We talked. She saw the cookies.

"Cookies?" she asked me.

"I know," I told her. "I shouldn't be rewarding her."

"No, you shouldn't be. The alpha dog doesn't put up with such behavior. Why do you let her get away with it?"

"I guess I don't do anything right."

Nina ignored Holly. She walked to the kitchen and offered me some water and a chair. I must have looked ragged. The dog followed behind us, trotting along as if she wasn't in deep trouble with me, as if nothing had happened. She lay down on the cool floor near the two chairs where Nina and I sat and talked.

When I left, I asked if I should say goodbye to her. Holly wagged her tail and smiled at me, giving me the "golden guile," the charm that melted my heart.

"No, just leave her, just go."

I said, "What do I do?"

Nina said, "Go home. Forget about her. Go take care of yourself."

Forget about her?

I SAT IN THE empty house. Holly's favorite chewed-up toy cougar was on the floor near the sofa. I didn't bring it with the rest of her things. She loved Cougar, slept with him, carried him around the house in her mouth, and I felt the regret of her loss as my own. I sat on the sofa looking out the window at the mallards on the lake. It seemed strange to me that the sun was still shining. How could this day continue in its brightness? I heard the voices and laughter of children playing through my open window. Everything seemed to continue as it was. The ducks were swimming as if nothing had happened. I wondered why there was always loss, and why I couldn't get anything right, and why I failed at every close relationship.

And now surely I had failed at the most primal relationship of all, the one with the dog of my dreams. My demons had been unleashed in the form of this monster I had created, a monster that would attack me. I emitted the smell of fear that even my dog recognized, the smell of weakness that the sharks in my life had gone after, like blood in the water.

I folded up all of her bedding from the outside back deck where she liked to stand guard at night. I tossed them into the washing machine and turned on the cool water, watching the machine fill until all of my dog's pads and colorful covers were underwater. The house was empty as death except for the sounds of the churning action of the washing machine.

I THINK ABOUT THOSE *black lacquered and flowered Chinese boxes, one placed inside the next one, each one larger than the one inside it. No matter how much growing I do, I still find myself in a box; maybe it is larger, but still I am imprisoned. If I grow and learn, and work very hard, and ask for nothing, and solve my own problems, maybe I will be better. But whenever I look around, there are still four walls, and I am still confined. It always feels like the same Chinese box. Am I here in the same box, facing the same failures again, this time with my dog?*

"I, who had had my heart full for hours, took advantage of
an early moment of solitude, to cry in it very bitterly.
Suddenly a little hairy head thrust itself from behind my pillow
Into my face, rubbing its ears and nose against my face
In a responsive agitation and drying the tears as they came."

–Elizabeth Barrett Browning (1806-1861)

Living with a Therapy Dog

AFTER TWO WEEKS OF rehab at Auntie Nina's, Holly appeared submissive and obedient. She had learned her place in the pack. She was not the leader. But just as with children I had counseled who showed improvement until they were returned to the same dysfunctional environment, the "good" behavior slipped back into the familiar just two days after she returned. It seemed that Holly and I were still in process, or I should say I was still in process. Holly had shown me that she could change. The question remained, could I?

I needed to respect myself before I could ask her to respect me. I knew for sure that she was sent to me for a reason.

Holly's patients were not the only recipients of her healing energy. There were intimate moments when she touched my deepest soul. Anyone who has ever fallen in love with a dog may experience an intimacy deeper than any they have known. They may also come nose to nose with frustrations. Dogs are not subtle in their needs and desires. They take us on a journey where we can discover a great deal about ourselves

Holly taught me about leadership. She also taught me about

love—by helping me to understand that loving her was not just about giving her kisses and affection and treats. It was about giving her what she actually needed, what all canines need—a strong leader. In fact, they require one in order to be calm and happy and obedient. Since I had problems asserting myself in all my relationships, this one was par for the course.

When I came home, it was I who went directly to her to demonstrate my affection instead of letting her come to me and shower me with the adoration that dogs are famous for bestowing on their masters. It seemed as if I needed her more than she needed me. I thought my role was to cater to this animal I adored. I thought you were supposed to give them choices. "Would you like to go out and play now? Would you like to eat now?" My behavior was submissive to her importance in my household. But Holly changed all of this for me. And there was no mistaking her message.

Anytime I didn't show her that I was the boss, she took over that role, sometimes being downright disobedient: not coming when I called her or barking aggressively at strange dogs on the street or in the park, as if she was the alarm system in charge of pack security. This display was not what I wanted from my dog. I felt embarrassed. I worried that another dog would take offense at her barking at them, and attack her. Holly would never bite anyone, it was all bravado, but her warning signals could trigger a dispute.

At the hospital I lived in terror of this misbehavior showing up. I turned the corners of corridors cautiously holding my breath for fear we would accidentally encounter another therapy dog and she would aggress. This kind of behavior would not be tolerated. Our days as a therapy team would come to a screeching halt. We would never work in the hospital again. I lived on the edge of danger.

I had a lot to learn about leadership. I learned that I was too soft. Once she jumped into the lake in front of our condo and swam after the ducklings, knowing I couldn't reach her, and defying me to catch her. The more I called and yelled her name, the farther away she swam and the more alarmed I became, as she was a predator and the baby ducks were surely prey. I feared for their safety and was furious that my great therapy dog didn't respond to my frantic calls.

Hearing my hysteria, several neighbors came outside to view in broad daylight my loss of control of this recalcitrant animal. One of them, Joe, stood at the edge of the lake and called "Holly!" in his deep male voice. She swam over and climbed out of the lake, shook off the water, and bounded over to greet him with sheer joy. I saw this and knew I wasn't commanding the respect from her that I craved.

The relationship with my dog resonated to other relationships in my life where I had allowed myself to be used or abused. When she "protected" our pack of two and took the dominant role by barking at strange dogs, I realized that I needed to be stronger, that I had to dominate her rather than the other way around. When she didn't come to my call, I knew my authority was lacking. In fact, this was her way of insisting that I become more assertive and in the course of her life, particularly in our work together, I reached a level of confidence I'd never had before in any relationship. Holly wouldn't let me get away with less than I could be. She needed me to be in charge of her, and in charge of my life. She let me know in no uncertain terms, and through acts of disobedience, that she needed me to set boundaries for her. She needed for me to become the leader of our pack of two. She was turning into a great therapy dog because, in the hospital setting, I took charge. It turned out that she was my therapist too. But there was one thing that never changed.

I was always in love with her. At night I would sit upstairs in the loft in front of the computer screen writing my stories and answering e-mails. I was not alone for long. By the time the screen had lit up and welcomed me musically, I heard the soft pad of my dog climbing up the stairs to be with me. Expecting her arrival, I left a sheepskin mat on the wood floor under my computer desk. Holly sprawled out on the soft fleece and stayed with me for the rest of the night while I worked. She lay at my feet contentedly, either snoozing or staring off into space in a meditative state, eyes half closed. Curled up on her side, she sometimes fell into a deep sleep, rolling over onto her back with her legs spread and her white furry belly vulnerable. With one hand I reached down and touched her head. Sometimes I stroked her tummy as she stretched out to give me all of her underpinnings. Softly she wakened and looked up at me with almond eyes and smiling open mouth. Her beauty was invasive as it moved right through my body and soul and calmed me. She felt my relaxed energy and closed her eyes going back to her dreams. These were moments when I felt very connected to her and to my life with her.

I was the most touched when she sat up and lay her sweet head in my lap. The weight and warmth of her relaxed me. I looked into her brown eyes, felt her trust, and knew we were communicating on a level beyond any human connections I've ever had. This must be the same healing energy that her patients experienced. I'd like to think she learned it with me. But I suspect it just came with Holly, just as with all the other therapy dogs.

Sometimes she sat on my foot. I found this charming though I learned some of this was a dominant gesture, to hold me there. If she was holding me there, it was fine with me. I never wanted to leave.

Working as a therapy team is socially acceptable, even admirable. But there is an entire population that considers the level of uncompromised devotion between human and animal close to pathological. Even friends that loved and supported me considered my animal connection not a "real" relationship.

Having dinner with a friend one evening, I noticed that it was five o'clock and started gathering up my things to leave. "I need to get home to walk Holly," I said.

Her response was meant to be helpful, but it startled me. "Maybe you can find a relationship with a person that would fulfill you."

True, everyone knew I had not made a success out of my marriages, even though I tried a few times. But I didn't dream that my deep connection with Holly was instead of a human relationship. This loving friend didn't get it, and she wasn't the only one.

While visiting my family in Florida, I couldn't stop talking about this great Golden Retriever who waited at home in Los Angeles for me. Sitting in the back seat of my brother's car, I heard my sister-in law comment casually to no one in particular, "Me…I'm not into animals, I'm into people."

I wanted to say, "But people are animals, a different species, but animals first." I said nothing, and felt put down for my loving "just a dog." I wanted desperately to say, "I like animals better than some humans." But I didn't say that either.

Many people think you're strange or fanatical for having these feelings. I found it safer to share negatives about Holly, telling stories of when she was disobedient, or when she tested the limits to see what she could get away with. I had no problem sharing those stories. Everyone had heard of the time at five months old when she ruined our first Thanksgiving together by jumping onto the dining room table, grabbing the turkey off the platter, and scampering away with it in her mouth. Everyone was amused by her antics. This was acceptable to share.

But I felt vulnerable in saying how much I adored this dog. It embarrassed me. It wasn't normal to love an animal so deeply. So I kept these feelings to myself. At the same time, I struggled to say out loud the things I feared would alienate me from the so-called sane world. "I'm nuts about this dog, she is the world to me, she is the love of my life." I gave myself permission to feel the intense pain over the impending loss that I knew was inevitable. I couldn't imagine a life without her. I let myself have this experience and stopped apologizing for my love of "just a dog."

I would have to accept myself just the way I was: in love with a Golden Retriever.

Holly's Plane Ride

"THIS IS MY FIRST dog," she said, smiling as we followed her through the boarding gate and onto the aircraft. The flight attendant seemed cheerful enough about it. Why was I so worried? My hair was soaked with perspiration. I felt like a criminal.

For weeks, I had waded through all the necessary paper work. Having first spoken with the FCC about their regulations for traveling with a dog, I then submitted Holly's registration as a therapy dog along with her photo I.D. from UCLA. It was stated in small print that if the handler, or trainer who was *not* handicapped, needed to transport an 'assistance dog' (Holly was really a therapy dog—this was a stretch) and had veterinary clearance, they were allowed to travel in the cabin. I said, "Bingo, that's us." We qualified! This was 1997. Never would we get away with this today in 2007. Nor would I ever be foolish enough to try. I felt guilt over smuggling her into the cabin, and maybe transgressing on the rights of a legitimate 'service' dog. I struggled with this for a long time.

I even did a walk-through a few days earlier to introduce Holly and the airport to each other. We practiced riding the escalator up and down until she got over her legitimate concern that putting her paws on a moving floor was not a great idea.

I had been honest about our qualifications. I said right from the start that I was not a handicapped person, but that my dog worked with psychiatric patients at UCLA's Neuro-Psychiatric Hospital. I explained that I was her trainer, handler and owner. All true. Not a false word. But I fudged a bit on the necessity for traveling with her. In the FCC requirements, transporting a working dog and handler was acceptable if the goal was a training program for the dog in another state. Marcie, a friend in Orlando, was a dog trainer who graciously offered to entertain us for a few days. I did stretch the truth a bit by asking my veterinarian to write a letter stating that we were flying Holly to Orlando for 'training' for the special work she did at UCLA. Well, most of it was absolutely true. We did visit Marcie, and training was unavoidable in her home. But the real reason for going to Florida was to introduce Holly to my ninety-five-year-old father before he died.

My dad had never seen my dog, and it was unlikely he'd be traveling to Los Angeles. He lived in West Palm Beach, and my plan was to fly directly to Orlando, stay with my friend, the "dog trainer," rent a car, and drive the few hours to WPB. Putting Holly in baggage was out of the question. I had heard too many horror stories about the risks and accidents, the lost dogs, and problems with temperature control. I would never consider putting any living thing in this risky environment. Flying was dangerous enough. Holly had to travel with me or we couldn't go.

My father was not particularly an 'animal person' and had more than once screwed up his face as he told me he didn't like cats. I had several cats at the time. I was accustomed to his disapproval of things. He would say, "I don't like cats—but dogs—I like." I noticed how he lit up when he spoke of his childhood dog, Spot. He said the dog never left his side, even jumping into the East River after he fell or was pushed in at the age of seven.

So that was my rationale for all of this trouble. I wanted to offer my father this one last gift; do something for him that he would like, even love, and of course get his approval—I would bring him my dog.

I arrived at the airport early, taking a friend along for support and a ride home if we were turned away at the gate. I couldn't imagine being allowed on the plane with this dog when I was clearly not handicapped. It crossed my mind to wear dark glasses and put a harness on Holly that I could hold onto, but that would be stooping even lower than I could do. I reminded the people at the check-in desk that I was boarding with a dog. Holly stood right there with me in the line. It was also noted on the ticket. No one seemed upset or too concerned. It was looking good, but still my hands were clammy. They told us we would board first along with the handicapped, the small children, babies; and anyone that needed special assistance. We waited in the boarding area. People stared at this uncrated dog, but I doubt if anyone believed she was actually getting on *their* plane. Holly lay at my feet, perfectly behaved, and watched with interest as the stream of people eyed her. Keeping a low profile with a large Golden Retriever was not easy. If she stood up to greet someone, I told her to "settle" and she lay right down again at my feet. Her obedience training was working. I wasn't about to call any more attention to her than was necessary.

Entering the airplane, we were seated in coach in the first aisle that had a bulk-head window seat, so there'd be no one in front of us. Holly lay on the floor curled up as tight as she could against the bulkhead wall. My feet rested on her back. Although we were cramped, we managed the tight squeeze until a woman sat down in the empty aisle seat next to me. 'Darn,' I thought. Holly needed all the floor space she could get. The woman looked down at the dog. Holly's broad tail twitched from side to side. The woman's feet were out in the aisle.

It was just my luck that out of all the people on this aircraft who would have enjoyed having a dog at their feet, I would be seated next to the one person who didn't. She glared at my Golden Retriever lying innocently on the floor. Holly, in her usual good humor looked up at the woman, gave her the golden guile, tail wagging, ready to make a new friend.

After the initial shock, and untouched by Holly's charm, the woman yelled, "I'm not flying with a dog in the plane. Get this damn dog off my plane." Oh dear! We had almost made it 'scot-free.' The airline attendants scurried, looking for another seat for her, as they tried to calm her down. Yelling was not allowed on their aircraft. They moved her out of this row as quickly and quietly as they could, while she continued to rant. This was their first dog on-board and they were almost as nervous as I was.

I tried to relax. People still boarding the plane walked by without noticing Holly lying under my feet. I was grateful she was not a barker. She was behaving like the working dog that I needed her to be.

The next hurdle was a walk-through by the captain. He apparently had not been apprised that there was a canine passenger on his flight. He came to an abrupt stop at my aisle. My heart pounded. I thought now we were going to get thrown off this plane. He raised both eyebrows and opened his mouth before he spoke. "What is going on?" he asked me. Clearly I was neither blind nor paraplegic. I stammered, "She was cleared for this already." I showed him my paperwork which stated that I was traveling with my 'assistance dog'—that stretch of the truth again. With shaky hands, I pulled out my Delta Certification papers stating she was registered with them. I yanked at her neck collar to show him the UCLA I.D. she wore with her picture on it. I also had purchased a maroon Delta Society vest for her to wear to be sure she looked official. Holly appeared friendly and benign as she gazed up at this man in the uniform, swishing her tail back and forth on the floor. But still he didn't respond to her appeal. He stepped away to talk to one of the flight attendants, the same one who had so cheerfully chosen the bulk-head row for our seating. He came back to my aisle and frowned, or scowled at me; I wasn't sure which. I held my breath, certain that the jig was up. He mumbled something incoherent, threw up his arms, and walked back to the flight-cabin.

We were going to Florida. The flight attendant began the demonstration for seat belts, oxygen, and exits and we were instructed to "always provide oxygen for yourself before your child." She didn't say anything about dogs. I thought I would probably give oxygen to Holly first. The 'Fasten your seat belt' light went on, preparing us for take-off. I finally exhaled! Would my father be happy? Would he be pleased that I brought my dog to see him?

As the plane began to move down the runway with increasing speed, the entire floor vibrated and roared underneath Holly's body. She stood up and looked for an escape route. I firmly told her "down "and "stay." Don't tell me that after all the trouble to get her on, that she wanted out of this plane. But she did what she was taught; she lay down even as her legs trembled.

Within ten minutes, we were airborne and she settled down to sleep. The worst was over. She slept through most of the flight except when the passengers came by with their cameras wanting a picture with her. They said it was their first plane ride with a dog. Always anxious to please, she posed with each passenger. I pulled out her photo album to show her lying in bed with her patients in cardiac care. Her admirers oohed and aahed, as if she were a celebrity. I felt more legitimate, showing people that she really did work in the hospital. She was petted and fussed over as flashbulbs went off. These were the days before cell phone cameras or there would have been many more recordings of this event. Of course the exception was the one woman who had objected to her presence on the plane. I never saw her again. Perhaps she left the plane and demanded a refund.

We had a lovely time with Marcie and her black labs in Orlando. But the real reason for my trip was beginning to make me anxious.

I drove to West Palm Beach in a rented car with Holly lying on the back seat. We made it there in less than three hours. I found my Dad's gated community, located his building amongst identical looking structures and took Holly up in the elevator to the 3rd floor. My brother and sister-in-law had already arrived. They came every winter to get away from the New York freeze.

My father lived alone in a one-bedroom apartment in an assisted-living facility that resembled a resort with pool, golf course, and beautiful grounds. He didn't need to shop or cook or clean, which was perfect, since my mother had taken care of all these things for him until her death a few years earlier. His meals were served in the dining room with the other residents. I had taken the tour the last time I visited, without my dog. The door of his apartment was not locked, and I pushed it open and stepped in, followed by Holly. My mother's touch was everywhere in the room. He had kept her ornate French provincial furniture and glass credenzas with all the little ceramic curios and other clutter that she loved. He had kept her in the room.

Dad lay sprawled on the sofa, looking very Floridian in his striped Bermuda shorts and yellow tee shirt with the alligator on the pocket. The tv was on. I didn't think he could hear it, but it was on. I greeted and kissed Rob and Bernice and looked across the room at my father. Holly eyed him also and, ignoring everyone else in the room, she made a bee-line to his side. It was as if she knew she had come to see him. I always seem to forget that our animals usually know what our intentions are. They 'read' us, and know what their purpose is. Or maybe she just thought he was one of her clients. He looked a lot like the elderly men in senior rehab that she visited. She sat alongside the sofa and leaned into his body the same way she did with her patients. As if they were old friends, he patted her head and smiled.

When it was time to go to dinner, Dad said he would rather stay home with "the dog." I suggested he could feed her; and left her bowl of dry food in the kitchen. He looked confused as to how I wanted him to do this. I said "Oh, just walk into the kitchen, she'll follow you."

We came home about an hour and a half later to find both man and dog curled up together, asleep on the sofa. Her head leaned on his shoulder. My Dad had his arm around her. He opened his eyes, and smiled at me. "I like dogs" he said.

After that visit, our boring phone conversations changed. In contrast to the uncomfortable pauses and his inquiries about the weather in California, every conversation began with "How's the dog?" He never did remember her name, but he knew that I had a dog. We had a connection. And just in case I hadn't figured it out by now, he always reminded me that he "liked dogs."

The End of the Journey

You think dogs will not be in heaven? I tell you, they will be there long before any of us.

—Robert Louis Stevenson

IT'S SEVEN A.M., AND I am awakened by warm breath on my cheek and loud breathing in my ear. I turn toward the warmth, open one eye, and am inches away from a black nose, white muzzle, and whiskers close enough to tickle me. Holly's mouth is open, with her pink tongue protruding. She is panting into my face, without as much as a whimper or bark, for the morning hello. Standing next to my bed, she is the exact height to rest her chin on the edge of my mattress. We are eye to eye. She stares at me. This translates to "get up." She continues to watch me until I stir from under the covers. I delay this delicious moment by petting her and feeling the softness of her silken ears that are still honey-colored. I tell her, "Good morning, *seis kindt*."

I continue to stay submerged to the neck under my warm down comforter. Holly stares. She is relentless. This is our basic communication system, no barking, just eye contact. I am not annoyed that she has wakened me earlier than my usual 9:00 a.m. schedule. In the past she sensed when I was ready to get up. I never needed an alarm clock. She doesn't sleep in anymore. And no matter how early she appears at my bedside, I say, "Thank you, god, for another day with Holly." This is an amazing statement for someone who says, "I don't do god." But this is a time of crisis and I need all the help I can get—so I'll take my chances with god.

I roll out of bed to be with Holly. My bare feet and her soft paws pad across the wood floor into the kitchen for breakfast. She gets kibble laced with two tablespoons of heated canned pumpkin. I was told by a holistic veterinarian that yellow vegetables are good for managing diarrhea. She has had chronic inflammatory bowel disease since she was five months old. I have always believed it was triggered by the stress of repeated dog bites as my too-friendly young puppy gaily approached strange adult dogs on the street. I didn't have a clue that I should be protecting her. She was corrected severely for her trust and my ignorance. Nothing in the books I read on raising a puppy warned me to keep her away from older dogs. There were serious repercussions of those early attacks that would change the course of our lives together. We both learned some hard lessons.

I eat my oat bran flakes with a banana and rice milk. Later I will eat my yellow vegetables too, and for the same reason. Her stressors have become mine. We manifest the same reaction to stress and I, too, have developed g.i. issues. We both have diarrhea.

She follows me back to the bedroom, and stands in the doorway watching while I slip into the gray sweats lying on the wicker hamper. No time for make-up or hair. I cover up my face with oversized sun glasses and my uncombed hair with a wide brimmed hat. Down the stairs we go. I lace up my tennis shoes in the entry way, and grab her red lead hanging on a hook near the front door. I hold the lead open as she presents her neck to me, walking into the loop. Good girl!

I open the front door as she waits respectfully for me to exit and follows at my heels. By now we have both learned the order of things, the status of our relationship. I lead, she follows. It took us awhile to get this straight in our minds—years, in fact. Still, there are moments of hesitation or weakness on my part, and then she leads me. I have to know where I'm going. This may be the mantra for my life. When I'm confident, we're in sync. That's the way it is.

Today we are out for our morning walk around West L.A. College. The sun is shining brightly in a clear blue sky and another glorious day with Holly has begun. I am grateful for it.

The tennis ball bulges out of the pocket of my sweat-pants. I will toss it for her to retrieve when we reach the top of the dirt fire road across from the college. Her tail swings as she walks at my side. Her keen sense of smell alerts her to the treasure in my pocket and heightens her excitement. Sometimes I let her carry it in her mouth. She will chase that ball even if she has to limp after it. With the early onset of arthritis, the vet suggested no more running, just walks. I said that Holly would not understand and would despair without the joy of chasing her tennis ball. She would think she was being punished if I withheld her daily play time. I had to weigh the progression of the disease with the quality of her life. She lived to retrieve. It's who she was. I could never take that away from her. I never did.

When we reach the summit, I unhook her lead and stand facing her with the ball poised over my head. She backs up in a ready pose, alert, waiting, legs astride, mouth open, eyes fixed on the ball. I yell. "Get it!" and toss the ball as far as I can. She scrambles after it, hobbling but determined, scoops it into her mouth and trots back to me, dropping it into my waiting hand. She backs up into the same stance and is ready to retrieve again. We have played this game at least once a day for nine years.

AND THEN ONE MORNING there is no warm breath on my cheek. There is no sweet white face leaning on the edge of my mattress and no pleading eyes riveted on me. She is too stiff to stumble over to greet me. These days she sleeps on her own comforter, preferring to keep her vigil on the floor at the foot of my bed.

I get up without her bedside invitation, and gaze at her gorgeous, still golden body, sprawled diagonally over her crumpled green bedding. She looks up into my eyes, tail thumping the floor and mouth open, panting. "Let's get up, sweetheart." I gently pull her onto her feet. She flops over on her side. She can't stand. Her legs, arthritic since she was five, finally have given out at the age of nine. My dog is lame.

I wonder how I will get her down the stairs of my condo and out onto the grass to relieve herself. Standing on the top step and throwing a cookie down the stairs used to motivate her to scurry after it while she ignored the pain in her legs. She wanted the cookie and, being a retriever, would chase anything. But today I must coax and push and pull and lift her all the way to the stairs. She holds one front leg up in a bent position, and the other paw barely touches the floor. She hops on her back legs as I assist her. It's not the first time she can't walk.

Landing in the wrong position, or on uneven ground as she jumped to catch her obsession, the yellow tennis ball, often caused her to twist a leg, tear a ligament, or injure a tendon, but they always healed after a time of rest. This is different. This is degeneration due to advanced arthritis. This is not temporary and not a sports injury. It is the decline of old age—a premature old age. I learned to handle those injuries by wrapping a large bath towel or my sweat shirt around her middle, tying it at her waist and then pulling up on it to take the weight off her front legs. So I know what to do today.

We get to the stairs; she hops down the first two with me pulling up on the towel. But the pain stops her dead on the third step. I gently smack her rear the way one encourages a horse to move. I hate myself for this but I say emphatically, "You have to walk." At 65 pounds she is too heavy for me to carry down the stairs. She hops down two more steps, then freezes.

"I can't do it," I imagine her saying. My heart sinks. I lower myself onto the stair. She flops down next to me. We sit there together quietly for a moment. Holly's face turns toward me and she looks at me the way she does when she wants something: her tennis ball, a cookie, to lick the last trace of ice cream off my plate, or eat the crust of my pizza, or to go outside in a rain shower. I always know what she wants. This time the look in her forlorn eyes tells me she wants me to stop the pain.

I try to massage away the ache in those long golden legs with their swollen joints, the same legs that carried her in freedom and joy across parks, fields, beaches, and any open space, soft velvet ears lifted and open as if to propel the whole body and spirit in the poetic motion of life, flying with no limits, no boundaries, no endings, mouth laughing.

I bring her into the veterinary offices the next day to have her legs x-rayed. I already know that she has arthritis, as she often limps after her ball. But the surgeon insists on x-raying her legs and also her abdomen. "Golden Retrievers often have splenic tumors," she says. "It's very common."

I decide she is overly conscientious. "How foolish," I think. It's just that she's not able to walk, nothing more.

I wait in the examining room for them to bring her back from Radiology. The surgeon reports something suspicious in the abdominal x-ray and orders an ultra-sound. I think she is a little bit crazy, but agree to it. Dr. Farber, her holistic vet, carries her back after the ultra-sound. The look on his face scares me. He is deathly white. I say, "Something's wrong?' not believing for a second that this surgeon's wild ideas have any validity.

"She has cancer of the spleen," he begins, but before he can tell me the rest, I feel my feet give way from under me. I feel as if I will hit the floor. "I need to sit down," I tell him. I slump into a chair.

He says, "Sometimes tumors in the spleen rupture and the dog can bleed to death." He schedules her surgery immediately.

When they cut her open and remove the large tumor in her spleen, they discover two more cancers in her colon. After her surgery, I sit in the car alone, crying. I am afraid to go home without her, afraid I will never see her again.

I drive home terrified that something awful is happening to my precious girl. I have forgotten the cats who have been alone without me. The minute I walk into the living room I smell something foul. Stormy, my diabetic cat, has soiled himself and is a mess. He needs an emergency bath. I bend over Holly's tub to wash Stormy in warm water and hear the crack. Ouch. I can't straighten up. My back has bent me in half on the same day of the mal-surgery. I live the metaphor. I cannot stand because I cannot stand it. I am broken. I manage to towel-wrap the cat and let him go. Then, unable to stand up, I stagger slowly to my bed and lie down.

The following day, I arrange for my pet sitter to bring Holly home from the hospital. My back is in spasm. I feel helpless. Meryl has cared for Holly for nine years. I know that she is grieving too.

When they arrive at home, I am lying in bed unable to get up. Holly plops down in her bed and stays there. It feels like death in my bedroom. Meryl stands in the doorway and says the wrong words. She tells me to "prepare myself." I have never been upset with Meryl until this moment. I say, "I'm not ready." She says, "Well, you better get ready." This sounds so cruel to me. I am too angry to tell her that I am well beyond prepared. My life will end with this loss of all losses. Doesn't she know that I will die without Holly? Prepare yourself?

I struggle to understand why this is happening to my nine-year-old dog. We are not finished. Why is she being taken away from me? Have I failed? Am I still the bad child, the defective child who never did anything right? Is this my punishment?

Unable to walk the distance from the UCLA parking through the long corridors of the Neuro-Psychiatric Hospital, where for the last eight years Holly has proudly announced her arrival, greeting everyone in her path, tail wagging merrily, lifting a paw for a handshake and what can only be described as the golden smile. I face the cruel reality. She has been the quintessential therapy dog, the first canine allowed in the hospital and the demo dog for new volunteer teams. I retire her quietly and simply with a phone call to notify the PAC office, and then the call to the adolescent unit where we have worked for eight years. We will not be in this week.

These have been the most fulfilling years of my life. Holly and I are connected to these teenagers. They give a luncheon in our honor and cook it themselves. It is the only time I am there without her.

The kids from 2 South, NPI's Adolescent Psychiatry unit, personally serve my lunch to me: macaroni and cheese, a green salad and chocolate cake. I am the guest of honor. It is the most elegant luncheon I have ever attended. I sit with a group of adolescent boys and girls on long wooden benches with our knees touching under the table. I relish the homemade food they created, and we talk about Holly. Each child has a story to tell about how Holly helped them with their problems. I am amazed that they know her stories as well as I do. For years I kept a journal and documented all the dramatic anecdotes. I wrote about all the kids she helped to recover; about all her healing work. Now it's over. All we can do is remember.

Today, these are not psychiatric patients. They are just "our kids" remembering "our" dog. I am ceremoniously presented with a plaque in Holly's honor. They have decorated the frame with paper flowers surrounding her picture that is featured in the center. It is the photo taken on our last day at Malibu Beach, her last day playing in the surf, hobbling on three legs on the muddy shore chasing after her tennis ball. She posed for the picture, standing with her front paws on a rock formation, with the shoreline and the sea behind her, like a picture postcard saying, "Greetings from Malibu." Like many of the patients photographed for the last time with a therapy dog on their beds, this is the last picture taken of her. The plaque with this picture hangs in the Neuro-Psychiatric Hospital in honor and memory of the healing work she did there.

Even though she couldn't attend, the luncheon is for Holly. There are tears and laughter. I am losing my working partner, my companion, my golden girl. These children will never forget her. I will never forget them.

At home, Holly entertains those who come to honor her, and to say goodbye. Her beloved Auntie Kc, the director of the PAC program at UCLA who trained us to be the first therapy team comes to visit her. She lays on the floor with her arms around Holly, just as she has always done when we invaded her office in the hospital. Holly would roll over on her back and the professional director of a prestigious program would get on the floor and give her a bear hug. Today she does the same. And Holly purrs and hums softly from pleasure at the touch of Kc's hands on her body.

Other devoted friends come to the house when I notify them that the time is short. Her "Auntie Meryl," the extraordinary pet sitter, comes to say goodbye. She and I have resolved the argument about "prepare yourself." We both know it is now. And it is all about Holly. Kisses and hugs go on all day. Holly has done well and is being rewarded. She devours the affection and forgets about the pain as canines do so well. She smiles her famous golden retriever smile and gazes at her friends with those eyes that entrance us all. Meryl says, "She is my best friend; she got me through some tough times." I didn't know this.

That night I keep a dim light in the room so that I can see if the nose bleeds start again. She has had cortisone injections in the knotty joints in her legs, codeine pills for pain, and morphine packs that slowly release painkillers, but still she pants and doesn't sleep. Panting is the way that dogs express their pain. I hold her in my arms and massage her legs. She will need a new morphine pack tomorrow. She had nose bleeds a few days ago that would not stop. I carried her to the car at 7 a.m. with blood covered towels wrapped around her face. Applying pressure did not stop the bleeding. My bedroom walls and carpeting are covered with rust-colored stains.

She was hospitalized for two days until the bleeding was cauterized. They don't know what caused the nose bleeds; maybe it was the pain medication. We are treating advanced degeneration in the joints of her legs. The surgeon is amazed she can stand at all.

A new ultrasound reveals that the cancer has returned. Now it is in her abdominal area. She weighs 65 pounds and I cannot carry her anymore. My back hurts. We are both in pain. I have not slept more than a few hours in weeks.

At 4 a.m. she seems to be quieter, so I crawl into my own bed, exhausted and sleep deprived. I drop into a numbness for about an hour. The sound of loud breathing close to my face jolts me awake. I open my eyes. She is staring at me. She somehow managed to get up and drag herself over to the edge of my bed, to the place she used to waken me quietly every morning by breathing into my face. Today when she looks into my eyes, I know exactly what she wants. She continues to stare. Holly has learned to make eye contact for everything she wants. I am the key to fulfilling all of her needs. I look into those brown soulful eyes, and I have no doubt of what she is asking for.

She wants me to stop the pain.

PART IV

THE FINAL GIFT

The Final Gift of Love

"Okay, I will help you." I will keep my word. No crying, no sympathy. No pity. I must act normal. It is just another day, another trip in the car to see Dr. Farber. I look in the mirror at my blank face, eyes puffy without sleep, without make-up, and put on some cologne. I'll smell normal to her when we go out. It's just another day.

My calm demeanor assures Holly that she is safe, that nothing terrible is going to happen. I am providing normalcy for her, though it is not what I feel. Inside my body there is seething hot pain. There will be time to grieve, to scream and pound my chest and pull my hair. But not now.

All of the years of struggle, of loss, of feeling unloved, of living in fear of loss, have brought me to this moment. Today I am offering my beloved Holly Go Lightly, my final gift of love...a peaceful death, without terror or trauma or hysteria. It's the least I can do.

I get dressed, and wait for 7 a.m. to call the veterinary offices. All the doctors are busy with their morning rounds. It is after 9 a.m. when I get a call back. "Is she going to get better?" I ask her internist. "No," he says. I take a deep breath and am quiet, for I know the next answer before I ask. "Am I prolonging the agony?"

I leave a message for Dr. Farber to call me when he comes in. Dr. Farber has given her acupuncture and positive energy for a year. She follows him everywhere, without a lead, even into the dreaded surgery room, so deep is her trust. She will die in his hands. I will not let anyone else touch her. He calls at 11 a.m. He is reticent to help me with this decision. He says, "Maybe there is something the surgeon can do for her legs. The cancer has not invaded any organs yet. She might have a few more months." Now I am totally confused. I suspect he's having trouble letting her go. I tell him I'll speak to the surgeon.

She calls me at 1 p.m. I say, "She's still eating, she still responds to me, she's still alert, the cancer hasn't attacked any organs yet." She tells me, "The constant pain in her bent and swollen joints is more than arthritis, since she has not responded to any of the anti-inflammatory meds. It may be bone cancer to be causing this much pain. And as far as eating, she's a Golden Retriever. I have seen them eating and still wagging their tails down to their last breath. We would have to biopsy her legs to see if it's bone cancer."

"No, we will not do that," I say. "Please tell Dr. Farber I am coming in." It has been decided. I will keep my word. I will help her. No crying. No sympathy. No pity. I look in the mirror at my face without make-up, and notice my half eyebrows. I take an eyebrow pencil to draw in the missing brow line. It's just another day.

I help her hop on her back legs by tying a large sweatshirt around her middle and pulling up on it to keep the weight off her front legs. We go down the stairs one at a time. I have to lift her into the back seat of the car.

My friend Nina, who always comes through when my dog is in trouble, has offered to go with us. We drive up to her house as she is returning from walking her pack of five West Highland White Terriers. She is a slim young woman wearing light blue denim jeans and a tee shirt. Her curly blonde hair bounces as she leads the Westies on their little legs down the street toward us, with light leads in both her hands. It's a Westie parade as the sun lights up the pure whiteness of their fur and cars slow down to take another look at this pretty girl with the five cute dogs.

Miki, the oldest, has been Holly's best friend from the first day they wrestled in the park and bonded as puppies of four months old. As they matured, Holly tolerated all the hi-jinx that she would never allow with any other dog. Miki still acts like a puppy, full of playfulness and although the same age, Holly hasn't played with Miki for years, though she still enjoys her company.

When Nina sees us in the car, she brings the dogs into the house; all but one. She comes right back with Miki, opens the back door of my car and Miki jumps in next to Holly. They have traveled together many times, smashed up against each other and the other dogs, crammed into the back seat with Holly perfectly content to have Miki sitting on top of her.

Today is different. Maybe they know. Maybe there is the smell of illness, or medication, or the smell of pain. They greet and lick each other's faces as we watch with tears in our eyes.

It is a final farewell of good friends.

We change cars silently. Nina puts Miki in the house and drives us to VCA Animal Hospital. I call for a tech to come down and carry Holly upstairs. I ask him to place her on the floor, and the three of us are led down the hall into the "grief" room. I don't want her carried in. I want her to feel as normal as possible.

Just another day. Nothing to be afraid of or anxious about. Holly hops on her back legs while I pull up on the sweatshirt wrapped around her middle. She stops to greet the staff as she passes them in the hallway. Laura, a vet tech, looks into my smiling face over her glasses and glances at the Golden Retriever she knows so well.

I tell her quietly "Today is the day." And that's all I say. I am not crying. I don't want Holly to think something terrible is going to happen to her. We are simply here as we have been many times. But the staff has been alerted, and they all know. They stop to pet her. I smile and say hello to each one.

Laura tells me days later that she has never seen anyone bring in their beloved pet for euthanasia with the calmness and normalcy that she witnessed that day. She remembered that I had only said, "Today's the day." She remembered that I had smiled and said hello to everyone. And she tells me she was stunned. She says women come in clutching their dogs or cats in their arms, crying hysterically. I tell her, "I could never do that to Holly." I didn't feel brave, just determined that she not be stressed or afraid. It's the least I could do for her.

I knew about fear. I also knew about love. I would give Holly the love I always needed and craved. My final gift. My finest moment.

The grief room, so aptly named, is carpeted and dimly lit. There is a small love seat and two arm chairs; two lamps with soft pink bulbs, and an end table with a box of Kleenex. I have said goodbye to Charlie, Lorelie, Lancelot, and held friends in my arms while they held their dying animals. I have been in this room too many times.

When Dr. Farber comes in, Holly tries to get up to greet him. For the first time, he is not smiling. He does not kiss her on the nose as he usually does. I feel his grief and say, "Aren't you going to kiss her on the nose?"

"Of course I am," he answers. And I say what I always say, "Oh, if you knew where that nose has been." And he answers, "I do know." And kisses her squarely on her black nose.

I act cheerful, smiling and joking with him. He is morose. I had not realized how hard this is for the doctors who get attached until I see his long face and watery eyes. I feel as if I want to help him through this. He inserts the catheter in her leg and leaves us, saying to let him know when I am ready. Is he kidding? I want to say, "Never." I will never be ready. Instead I say I'll call him.

My daughter arrives. We sit around and visit with Holly. Nina goes to the candy machine and buys her a chocolate-covered peanut butter bar. I say, "Oh, I should have brought her rice cakes. She can't eat that." Nina says, "Marian, she won't have diarrhea." Holly has lived on rice cakes for treats because of her bowel disease. She never has candy. I don't really get that she will not have diarrhea ever again. Her auntie Nina gives her two candy bars. Holly cannot believe her good fortune and wolves them down happily.

One by one, members of the staff come into this room to pet her and say goodbye. She has been coming here for nine years, and the staff know and adore her. Holly has a relationship with everyone. She is lying on her stomach on the sheepskin pad I brought in from the car, with her head up, looking around, alert and interested in watching the parade of visitors. She thinks she's at a social event, which is just what I intended. The staff members kneel down on the floor and hug and kiss her. She wags her tail and smiles her golden smile for each of them. I find it strange that everyone is saying goodbye, like some sort of ritual. I know in my heart she is coming home with me. She always comes home with me. She is my dog.

Don't these people know she is coming home with me? I would never leave her.

Everyone is visiting, and talking in this lively room. No one is crying. Holly socializes with everyone, and is having a good time as the center of attention. She loves this. Someone steps in and reminds me that Dr. Farber has to catch a plane at 7:00 p.m. Have I forgotten the horror of why we are here? It is nearly 5:00. I say,

"Okay, please call him." My daughter gets up and walks out of the room. I think she is fearful of death since her father died when she was fourteen. She avoids hospital visits and funerals. Nina asks to stay. She has been Holly's auntie, friend and trainer for nine years. I say, "Yes, stay."

Dr. Farber arrives, looking like he just lost his best friend. I have never seen him upset before. He has been my support system for the last year, always smiling, always keeping things positive and hopeful for me and for Holly. He attaches the IV tube filled with fluids to the catheter in her leg. I ask about first giving a tranquilizer, as I know that valium usually helps to relax the animal before the overdose of anesthesia that will stop the heart. He says yes, valium is already set up in the IV tube. Again, he asks me if I am ready.

I think *never*. I say, "Yes." He releases the clamp that starts the flow of valium through the catheter into her vein. I lie down on top of Holly, covering her body with my own, feeling her heart beat, and letting her feel mine. I want to shield her from all of this.

Let it go through my body first.

Dr. Farber holds her head in both of his hands as the valium is drained from the catheter into her body, and she sinks into a sleepy and relaxed state, her head dropping to the side of his arm where it rests. Now the pink drip of anesthesia begins. It lasts only a few seconds. I hold back the rush of emotion until I feel her leaving her body. I don't want her to hear this. And now as if the clamp on my emotions has been released as well, all of the wrenching sobs of a life time, expel from the guts of my body.

All that has built up for the last eight months since her diagnosis and probably all of my life begin to climax, building up louder and deeper without any self consciousness, without any concern for anyone else in the room, or outside in the hallway, until the offices and examining rooms and surgical areas and kennels are filled with my agony. It is primal, it is all of the hurt and pain and grief that exists in the world, flooding out of me, and there is no stopping it.

I hear someone else in the room crying softly. It is Nina. My face is buried in Holly's fur. She is quiet but seems to be asleep. I think I feel her heart. I stop weeping and look up. Dr. Farber is now leaning weakly against the wall. I say, "She's still breathing." He assures me she is not. He bends down with his stethoscope to listen, and says, "There is no heart beat." He asks me if I want to stay longer. "No," I tell him. Do I want her tail? I never heard of such an idea. I say, "Yes." Nina carefully cuts a beautiful golden plume of fur, keeping it in one piece, and ties it with a ribbon. I put it in my purse, walk to the door and leave her there on the floor.

I go home without my dog.

October 24, 2002: *Outgoing voice mail message:*

"To my friends calling to inquire about Holly : Today I made the agonizing decision to give Holly my final gift of love by allowing her gentle spirit to leave her beautiful golden body and continue the journey of healing for which she was sent to us. She had a beautiful death, assisted by her beloved Dr. Farber, with all the courage, dignity and style with which she lived; surrounded by love and gratitude. With bliss, she died in his hands. She sends you all her steadfast unshakable love with reminders that: *All we have is love. Love is all there is.*

Your messages are appreciated."

And in my breast
Spring wakens too.
And my regret
Becomes an April violet,
And buds and blossoms like the rest.

In Memoriam...Alfred Lord Tennyson

Reprise

I NEED MUSIC AND words in my life. It is my spiritual sustenance. Sometimes I forget this. But then I remember the little girl who sang herself to sleep at night. I would go through all the songs in my head, the show tunes, the songs my mother taught me, all the lyrics of my life, until I fell asleep. My parents must have heard me singing, and perhaps knew when it was quiet that the concert was over.

I remember the moments that changed me as a person. I remember—when my father stopped loving me, and when I was so depressed I wanted to jump in Sheepshead Bay in Brooklyn and drown. Strangely, I have an early memory of my father lovingly pushing me in a stroller along the Bay while the docked houseboats swayed and creaked.

The most appalling thing about me is that I may not remember names and dates and places, but I remember every rocky word ever spoken to me and every warm touch withheld. I have memorized crucial conversations. They are imprinted as staged scenes in my life with bright lights, action and dialogue. This gets me into trouble with longtime friends when I quote back to them verbatim, often words they want to deny were ever spoken. They say, "I don't remember that." I say, "I do." The right words! I would remember the wrong words forever. "Department of Correction? I have a bad child. Can you come and pick her up?"

I remember being a five-year-old child stored alone in the back yard of the two-family brick house where purple irises and white rose bushes bloomed in the back yard. Up and down, back and forth, I rocked my doll carriage containing my only companion, a pink-cheeked baby doll covered to her neck with a baby's soft receiving blanket and wearing a lacy white bonnet tied under her chin.

I don't remember the names of most of my teachers or the kids I went to school with. Yet I remember well the 3rd grade teacher, Mrs. Slavin, with her Buster Brown hair cut and pink slip that stuck out an inch or more under her shapeless dress. She called me up to stand in front of the blackboard because I was bad. I had talked. I felt the blood rush to my head in humiliation. Oh yes, I remember her.

My mother also told me I was bad every time I didn't eat her food and propped up my sleepy head with my elbows on the rosebud oil cloth that covered the kitchen table. She told me I was bad every time I had an original thought or when I wanted to choose the purple taffeta dress with the big bow in the back instead of the boring pale cotton one she had picked out.

It was my brother who taught me to write and recite words when I was eight and we wrote funny scripts together. He didn't remember that he was my first writing teacher. But I do. We impersonated the comics on the radio shows and even sang the commercials. We performed the skits in our play room in the basement and charged all the neighborhood kids two cents admission. When I was ten I remember dancing around the ping pong table in a long red skirt while the record on the turntable played "Lady of Spain". We charged a nickel for that show.

I remember the words he spoke to me when I was frightened.

"Whatever happens, this will be over tomorrow." When I was scared, I learned to picture myself waking up in my bed the next day safe and warm under the quilts. Those words helped me through many shadowy terrors and days of bloody agony. I would say, "It will be over." He may not remember, but I do.

I remember every single word David said to me, and every word he did not say. I remember every time he left me and every time I thought I would die without him.

Words are important. I memorize them. I keep them with me in my fuzzy head and in my broken heart. Sometimes they are all there is. Why would I forget the words I need to remember?

Most of all I remember Holly Go Lightly, the dog I waited for my whole life.

I remember that through every great moment in my life—joyous, tragic, hurt, celebratory—there was a song that highlighted the event and gave it a voice, a heartbeat, a rhythm.

Those songs were the music of my soul. They resonated in my head, my heart, in all my body movements. It was primal, sexual. It was Sinatra singing *"All the Way"* the first time I fell in love with David, or when we found each other again years later and listened to Frank sing, "Love is lovelier, the second time around." I felt Sinatra in the pit of my stomach. As someone said at his funeral, "His music was the soundtrack of my life."

WHEN HOLLY WAS A puppy, I sang to her. Each night after I fed her, I removed her red leather collar with all its jangling I.D. tags, signaling to her that she was to be groomed or bathed. She always wore her tags indoors just in case she accidentally exited from the house. Years of doing rescue work finding stray and lost dogs without a single tag of identification taught me this precaution. My worst fear was losing her, so the tags stayed on except for bath and grooming time. Relieved of the dreaded bath, she lay down on her sheepskin pad on the kitchen floor.

Under the kitchen's bright fluorescent ceiling lights, I carefully brushed and combed her soft as down, still very blonde puppy coat without missing a single tangle. She didn't particularly care for the tug of the comb. If I tugged too hard, she lifted her upper lip in a grimace letting me know it was hurting her. She was actually warning me. This was a preview of the primal "wolf" face I would later come to know. I didn't correct her for the hostile warning. She was too little and cute. I sang to her as a distraction while I worked through the snarls in her wavy coat. Then I would let her rest while I lay down next to her propped up on my elbows looking into her eyes. The words of an old song seemed to come straight out of my unconscious. In the film *The Blue Angel*, Marlene Dietrich sang *"Falling in Love Again"* with the German accent and sultry tones she was so well-known for. I remembered only some of the lyrics, but the words came pouring out of me with such emotion that Holly lay very still with those almond eyes fixed on me, no movement, no tail wagging, just there in that moment with me. I decided she liked this song because I sang it from my heart.

> *Falling in love again, Never wanted to,*
> *What am I to do? I can't help it!*

I added, "*Hoo hoo,*" as a tag line, and I think she liked that part the best. I felt her smile during the "hoo hoos." As I listened to the lyric I was singing, I became conscious of the words and their meaning. I had not trusted myself to fall in love with anyone since Dave left me more than twenty years ago. Yet I had fallen in love again. But this time I was safe.

Holly would never leave me, except in death.

I recalled another verse:

Love never was my game,
Play it as I may, I was made that way,
I can't help it!

And again, "*Hoo hoo.*" I wasn't sure this lyric was correct, but that's how I sang it for all of the nine years Holly shared my life. She was an appreciative audience and avid listener, looking straight into my eyes and knowing I sang it to her, and was in love with her. She had to know that. My feelings were in synch with my words, and she had to know that as well. So we had 'our song,' just as my mother and I had our song.

WHEN I WAS A child, my mother taught me to sing "Till We Meet Again." She would harmonize while I sang the melody, and this always threw me off and I'd lose the tune and join her in the harmony. I never did get it right. She would stop and look at me as I started singing her part. We laughed and started over again.

When she was dying, I sat on the edge of her bed every day for a week. I fed her ice cream, and Ensure and held her hand as we sang. The day before she died, we sang our song together for the last time. It was our final goodbye to each other. I always wanted to join her in harmony—in our lives as in our singing. But I always fell off the tune by trying so hard. I finally made that connection with her on the last day of her life. And this time I sang her song right on key without the distraction of the harmony. She tried to sing her part, but she was too weak.

In the end, I sang alone, in much the same way I had lived my life.

I listened closely to hear my mother's words. She had lung

cancer and was tethered to oxygen. Her voice was faint. I stayed squarely on the tune and didn't lose it, not this time.

> *Smile the while I kiss you sad adieu,*
> *When the clouds roll by I'll come to you,*
> *Then the skies will seem more blue,*
> *Down in Lover's Lane, my dearie,*
> *Wedding bells will ring so merrily,*
> *Every tear will be a memory,*
> *So wait and pray each night for me,*
> *Till we meet again.*

Those who knew me well, and perhaps even loved me, must have known of the vital importance of words for me—the right words. The most important words I ever said to my mother were, "Mommy, can I have a puppy?" "No dogs in the house," resonated throughout my life as the ultimate rejection of my needs, my wants, the refusal to see my loneliness. I doubted she ever knew how much those words meant. Now our time together was over. She was dying. I was going home, never to see her again, alive or dead. The words had been unspoken for fifty years. "Mommy, can I have a puppy? Please Mommy, I'll take care of it, I promise."

Like the final request of a dying man, I reached for hope. Can you, my mother, know who I am? Can you understand my longings, my passions, my dreams? Can I ask you to approve of me before it's too late? And in a flash I knew this was the moment. There would be no other.

"Mom, I'm getting a puppy."

She tried to lift her head from the pillow. "You always wanted a dog."

She remembered.

"What are you going to call it?'" she asked. I couldn't believe she wanted to know the name of my dog She was interested in me. Maybe she knew who I was.

"Holly Go Lightly," I said. And then reaching for the moon and the stars, I asked the question. "Do you like it?" I really meant, "Do you like me?"

"I don't have to like it, only you do," was the whispered answer. I was so accustomed to disapproval that I sank down in my chair. She can't do it, I thought. She was once again denying me her acceptance just as she had denied me the puppy I longed for in my childhood.

Now, years later, when I re-play this scene, after a life time of struggles, and a dog who insisted in canine fashion that I become all that I can be and take charge of my life, I hear it differently. She was right. Only *I* had to like it. These were the only words she could have given me to set me free. I didn't need her approval, I only thought I did. I was the one who needed to approve of me.

Yes, I liked the name Holly Go Lightly.

My mother used to reminisce that the best time in her life was the year I was sick with asthma. We took the subway on Saturdays into the city to see Dr. Kugelmas, the Park Avenue allergist. It sounded as if she cherished my being sick and dependent. I hated that she needed me to be sick.

In looking back, I think I misunderstood that too. Perhaps her fondest memory was a time when we were together, just the two of us. For me, it was probably the best connection I had with my mother. Two women out on an adventure, away from restrictions and assigned roles, looking through the windows of fancy Madison Avenue stores at bridal gowns and fantasizing about a better life.

Anything was possible.

Mother's Day

So okay, I was not a perfect mother. My daughter figured that out all by herself when she was four years old. She said, "I wish you were a real mommy." And I said, "Honey, what is a real mommy?" She looked up at me and thought for a moment. "Well, you know, they stay home and make brownies."

I never did bake brownies. And I never stayed home either.

Now forty years later, Terrie is a performance artist using her life stories for material, so of course like it or not, I'm in her work. I go to all her stage performances, squirm in my seat when the word 'mother' comes up, even though she has sworn to me she'll never do "mommy dearest." This year she decided that it would be nice if I would perform a piece with her for a Mother's Day celebration at a local theater. She got us booked, printed flyers, and then on the night of her birthday, told me as a surprise, maybe as a gift, amidst giggles, "I'm going to make a performance artist out of you. I'm going to make you famous." I stared at her, no one at the table saw me smile or heard me say okay.

She reminds me that I said, "I guess I have to lose weight. But I never dreamed she would ask me to don a liartard and dance across a stage in tights in front of a hundred people. I'd have to lose more than weight for that. I am not a performance artist. I'm a writer, comfortable with putting words on a page, and not comfortable in front of an audience. Yet she didn't think twice about setting this up for a Mother's Day performance.

She told me that she wanted me to know who she was by introducing me to what she did. I said I didn't need to jump out of a window to know that I wouldn't like the fall. I said "I know who you are, you're the performer, I'm the prop. I should have said no before the fliers went out.

Two months later, and two weeks before Mother's Day, Terrie arrived at my house for the first rehearsal. She brought a tape recorder and asked me questions about my life, my mother and my childhood. She got me talking, telling her old stories while taping all of it. The questions became more personal, more probing. We were deep into my childhood. I needed to stop her.

I say: "I don't want to go there anymore. This isn't my show; it's yours. Let's hear from you now. What do *you* want to do? I feel myself getting angry.

"This is the way I work," she says. "I gather material, then I process it and see what I want to use. It's organic, I want to see what the possibilities are"

I ask her "So what are the possibilities, *you* tell me."

I'm feeling interrogated. She's crossed my boundaries.

She asks me what it is I would like to do.

"Sit in the audience." She laughs.

"You have to be onstage."

I say, "No, this isn't who I am, this is who you are."

"How can I get out of this?" I ask my friends. I feel anxious and I lie awake at night. My stomach is upset.

Second rehearsal. Terrie asks: "So how did you feel when I

asked you to be a performance artist?" I remind her again that she never asked me, that she told me.

I say to her: "What if this doesn't work, like maybe our working together is not one of your better ideas. Maybe you should do the piece alone."

She tells me we are booked together as a mother/daughter performance and that's how she got the theatre to agree to it. She tells me she will make it work. I say,

"But what if it doesn't work, do I have the option of getting out of this?"

"I'll make it work."

I yell, "You're not hearing me!"

She yells back: "I can't force you to do anything you don't want to do."

She doesn't say, It's ok, you don't have to do it. She is not going to let me out of this.

Now she wants us to rehearse in front of the mirrors in my bedroom. She takes my hand and leads me there. I can tell she thinks this is so cool because she's giggling again. She asks me to remember a time when I felt fierce.

I say, "I never felt fierce."

"How did you feel when you were leading groups at UCLA hospital?"

"Confident."

"Ok," she says" How would you express that confidence with your body movement?"

And that's when I say:

"No. I'm not doing movement on stage, you can't ask me to do that. I'll sit in the audience and watch you."

She says, "Mom, you can't. You have to be in the piece."

So I say, "Okay, let me sit on a stool on the side of the stage, and YOU do all the dancing."

And then my daughter gives me the line that reminds me of the brownies I never baked for her.

"Mom, you're killing my creative process." God forbid, I should kill her creative process. She asks me to put on a leotard and hose and show my legs to the audience. I say no. She's gone too far.

I say, "Why didn't you ask me to do that 30 years ago when I had good legs?" She tells me that she wants the audience to see what she had to grow up with; that her mother had showgirl legs and that she had horrible thighs. I have heard her berate her body image in her stage performances many times. She uses this as material. I know she thinks something is wrong with her body, with her looks, and finally with herself. I tell her I think it's sad that she feels that way. And now I share some memories with her.

"Terrie, when you were 16 and I was about your age, when we lived in the Marina, one day we were putting on swimsuits to go to the pool, and you took my hand and walked me to the full length mirror on the closet door, just like you did today. And you said, "Look at that."

I said, "What?"

You said, "There's something wrong when your mother has better legs than you do." Terrie says she doesn't remember this.

And then I relate an incident with my mother when I was 16 and we were walking down the street together. A car pulled up alongside the curb, and a bunch of guys rolled down the window and gave out a long low wolf whistle—at her, not at me. I stepped back and became invisible. Your nanny was about 46 then, wore no make-up, plain dresses, nothing provocative, yet it was clear they were looking at her, not at me.

And when I started dating, I would walk into the living room, after spending an hour on make-up and hair, and my dates never even looked up. They were sitting on the sofa enchanted with my mother, unable to tear themselves away. And finally I tell her about the time Nanny took me to see the allergist, Dr. Kugelmas when I was 14, and he said right to my face. "You're an attractive girl but you'll never be as good looking as your mother."

So I say "Terrie: this is universal, this is mother/ daughter stuff. If you had a daughter she'd think you were incredible. She'd think she could never measure up to *you*."

"Well, we'll never know, will we," she responds, and I know I've hit a nerve. So I tell her I wrote something when she first told me about this Mother's Day event. I say, "This is what I would say if I'm up on the stage with you."

She tells me it's ok if I read this, but only because I really want to, not exactly what she had in mind. She wants it to be conversational between us. I hear the word improv.

I say, "You better cue me, have prepared lines, and no surprises. I don't do improv." She hands me the transcription of the tapes she made. It's the dialogue between us; it's all there, even my protests. I say "Oh, this is good." It is amazing.

Third rehearsal; it is 2 days before the show. We meet at the gym in the yoga room. Now I tell her that I've not been sleeping, and that my g.i. problems have returned; the diarrhea is back. This time she hears me.

"Mom if this is making you sick, you don't have to do it. You're off the hook."

I say, "Too late, let's just do it and get it over with."

"But you don't have to do it," she tells me again.

By now I am resigned. I'm starting to find humor in all of this. Terrie's script from the tapings is really good. I understand what she did with the interviews. I see what she meant by organic, the script came out of our interaction. Maybe we can make this work.

She tells me she wants to sing on stage with me for a big

finish after we both reveal our legs. I say "Oh god!" She wants to sing my favorite Cole Porter song *Anything Goes*. I go home and download the lyrics and send them to her.

Last rehearsal. We meet at the theatre, stand together on the stage and practice singing *Anything Goes*. It's a tricky lyric and she can't seem to get the rhythm or melody right. She keeps going off key. Each time she loses it, I stop and stare at her. She laughs. We start again. She loses the melody. Terrie knows that I sang a special song with my mother and asks if I want to sing that.

I say, "Ok, but I might cry."

"Why?" she asks.

"Since I was a little girl, Nanny and I always sang our song together. She taught me the melody, and she would harmonize just over my part. But hearing her sing different notes always threw me off and I would join her harmony. When she was dying, I sat on the side of her bed and we sang *Till We Meet Again* for the last time. She could still sing harmony. But I struggled to stay on the melody."

Terrie starts to laugh out loud. "Oh, you too!" she says.

Then I read the piece I had written. I read it to her and she's smiling. I begin:

> "I used to wonder why Alcoholics Anonymous was more effective for treating alcoholism than psychotherapy. After going to an AA meeting, I figured it out. People get to stand up in front of the world and say: MY NAME IS JOHN and I AM AN ALCOHOLIC. And something happens, something changes. Today on Mother's Day, with my daughter present, I need to stand up in front of an audience and say:
>
> "My name is Marian and I was an imperfect mother struggling to be perfect by producing a perfect child. I didn't

believe I was good at anything. Why would I be good at mothering? Maybe if I could produce a perfect child, that would be good. Terrie, you were already perfect. You were born perfect. If you grew up thinking you could never please me, that you could never do anything right, and that there was something wrong with you, it was not you that was lacking. It was me.

"I carried a load of heavy rocks on my broken shoulders and gave them to you to carry. But your strength and your spirit were never broken, you carried them a long distance before you threw them away, a rock at a time, and stood up tall and beautiful, just the way you are, perfect."

TERRIE LOOKS AT ME a moment, then says, "i think it's going to work." I notice she has tears in her eyes.

Epilogue

HOLLY GO LIGHTLY, WITH the instinct and commitment of a retriever, carried a gift in her soft mouth and offered it for examination. But it was not a bird or live prey. She presented me with the gift of discovery. This dog had been unwilling to accept anything less than a calm, confident, and stable leader who understood she was a dog and not a child, and she had canine needs, very different from the emotional longings of humans.

Holly's gifts helped me to heal my life. I didn't recognize them as gifts at first; I saw some of them as "problems." I came to understand her behaviors were simply a reflection of my own needs, unresolved issues, and childhood injuries.

This awareness was *her* final gift to me.

Some people speak of an angel sitting on their shoulders, guiding and protecting them. I have always suspected this was just fantasy and comforting to us as an insecure species. And yet, each night as I sit at my computer and I write this book, there is an empty spot on the floor at my feet. Except it isn't empty. It seems to hold Holly's golden energy; which waits, tail swishing back and forth on the floor, ears perked up listening, eyes watching me, mouth parted with excitement, the same energy that readies for the release signal to go to work, to——

"Go say hello!"

Made in the USA
Middletown, DE
28 June 2015